REIKI for Beginners

Mastering Natural Healing Techniques

DAVID VENNELLS

MANJUL
Manjul Publishing House

First published in India by

MANJUL

Manjul Publishing House

• 7/32, Ansari Road, Daryaganj, New Delhi 110 002 – India
Website: www.manjulindia.com

Registered Office:
• 10, Nishat Colony, Bhopal 462 003 – India

Reprinted from
"Reiki for Beginners"

Published by Llewellyn Publications,
Woodbury, MN 55125 USA
www.llewellyn.com

This edition first published in 2019

ISBN 978-93-88241-49-6

Interior illustrations: Carrie Westfall
Editing and book design: Michael Maupin

Printed and bound in India by Thomson Press (India) Ltd.

For sale in India, Pakistan, Nepal, Burma, Bangladesh, Thailand, Sri Lanka, Singapore and Malaysia.

Just for today do not worry . . . Just for today do not anger . . . Honor your parents, teachers, and elders . . . Earn your living honestly . . . Show gratitude to every living thing.

— The Five Reiki Principles

Why learn Reiki?

Reiki is a simple yet profound system of hands-on healing, developed in Japan, that transcends cultural and religious boundaries. It is also a gentle, yet powerful path to personal and spiritual growth. Reiki can have a profound effect on health and well-being by rebalancing, cleansing, and renewing your internal energy system. Here are a few examples of how you can use Reiki either as a "hands-on" healing technique, or by setting mental intentions:

- To heal yourself and others physically, mentally, and emotionally
- For personal growth and developing compassion and wisdom
- To heal animals and plants
- To heal relationship problems at work or home
- To send healing energy to world situations such as wars and natural disasters, or local situations such as crime, unemployment, and poverty
- To complement and strengthen other therapies such as Aromatherapy and Reflexology
- To find new employment, a new house, car, or anything else
- To have a safe and swift journey while traveling
- To find a solution to a specific problem
- To calm yourself before going into stressful situations such as exams, interviews, or public speaking
- To always be blessed, guided, and protected

Author's Note

The author would like to point out that he is not a teacher of Buddhism, and that any advice given from a Buddhist perspective to support the practice of Reiki is simply something he has found helpful in his own experience of Reiki.

This book is not an authentic Buddhist text. Any reader interested in deepening his or her knowledge of Buddhism, or learning to meditate, should consult the information given in Appendices 1 and 2 of this book.

Other Books by the Author

Bach Flower Remedies for Beginners
Reflexology for Beginners

Contents

Acknowledgments

Special thanks to Dr. Mikao Usui for his gift of healing from within and above. Also to Dr. Chujro Hayashi and Mrs. Hawayo Takata, for bringing Reiki to the West and helping it to flourish.

Many, many thanks to my parents for their constant love and support.

Also to Reiki Masters Carlyn Clay and Padma O'Gara for their inspirational example, and to Mary Macintosh and Beryl Vale for their great kindness in introducing me to Reiki.

Sincere thanks to the following who have helped me in many different ways: my sisters Paula and Clare and their families; my godparents May, Jimmy, and James; friends Greg, Paul, and Paul; Kelsang Tubchen, Sam, and all those who have contributed to the making of this book.

Also, special thanks to all those who have looked after me and taught me, especially Venerable Geshe Kelsang Gyatso Rinpoche and Kelsang Khyenrab for their special teachings and blessings.

Though Earth and man were gone
And suns and universes ceased to be
And Thou wert left alone
Every existence would exist in Thee.

—Emily Brontë

Introduction

Writing this book has been a special experience, a great joy and a real privilege. Reiki has touched my life in many special ways and has given and continues to give me so much that it is hard to express in words how grateful I am.

There are now many books available on Reiki and no doubt many more will follow. It can be quite confusing for the beginner and the experienced practitioner to see through all this information to the heart, or essence, of Reiki, so it is important to remember that Reiki is basically a very simple, enjoyable, and experiential technique. Keeping our practice simple, learning from other practitioners, books, and—most importantly—our own experience is the key to successful Reiki.

Since Reiki came to the West from Japan, people's awareness of the roots of Reiki in the Buddhist tradition has been diluted. This is now changing rapidly as we learn more about the life of Dr. Mikao Usui, the founder of Reiki, and on how Reiki is practiced, as he originally taught it, today in Japan. This should not worry Reiki practitioners who are not Buddhist. We definitely do not need to be Buddhist to practice Reiki and we definitely do not need to be Buddhist to benefit from Buddha's teachings. They are both open to everyone, always.

Today, Reiki is combined with many different types of spiritual practice, other therapies and paths to personal growth, and there are new branches of Reiki arising as some Masters introduce their own ideas and techniques. Perhaps as a result of this the office of Western Grand Master is looking at ways of preserving and protecting the authenticity and clarity of the lineage and original teaching practices that came to the West via Reiki Master Hawayo Takata. With all these changes happening, the way forward can seem a little confusing! It seems that today many Reiki practitioners are looking for an authentic spiritual framework, form, or context in which to deepen their understanding and experience of Reiki. I became interested in Buddhism not long after becoming a Reiki practitioner and found that the practice of Buddhism and Reiki were very complementary. Practiced together, they both improved my quality of life tremendously while still allowing me to honor my Christian roots.

The motivation to write this book came from the wish to share the good health, sense of personal fulfillment, and deeper appreciation of life that I have gained from Reiki and Buddhism. I also felt that a simple guide to Reiki from a general Buddhist perspective might help Reiki practitioners, traditional and nontraditional, gain new and clearer insights in to their own Reiki practice and path toward personal growth.

I hope this book is helpful, and enables you to clarify, understand, and deepen your own experience of Reiki and become a little more whole, healthy, and happy along the way.

Preface: The Author's Story

One morning before I sat down to write, something happened that seemed very symbolic of my own first experiences with the healing power of Reiki.

On the window ledge in our kitchen there is a house plant in full bloom, with perhaps forty or fifty beautiful white flowers on stalks surrounded by green leaves all growing from a central bulb—a cyclamen. I had forgotten to water it for some time and noticed that all the flowers and leaves had fallen over revealing the bulb. It seemed to completely lack vitality and was obviously losing the will to live. I immediately gave it a good drink of water, a little Reiki, and hoped for the best.

When I returned to the kitchen about thirty minutes later, I was amazed to discover it had almost completely recovered! All the flowers and leaves stood up and pushed toward the light again. You could almost see a glow of Life Force Energy surrounding it. The change was swift, remarkable, and wonderful. I just stood there for a few minutes admiring this amazing natural transformation.

The gentle simplicity and power of this touched me in a way that made me clearly recall my own first experiences with Reiki. In fact it was like a key in my mind that revealed and reminded me of the magic of those first weeks and months. So many wonderful and awakening events have happened to me since then. It is now a real joy to come full circle and recall how I came to here from there!

Toward a Real Graduation

Until my early twenties, my life had been fairly normal. In recent years, since coming to Reiki, I began to remember my very early childhood touched with a sense of freedom, contentment, and loving protection that emotions and sensations of later life seemed to cloak with a vague sense of loneliness and isolation. Looking back now, the outside world did not seem to have the intention, understanding, or support system to encourage the potential of childhood. Perhaps this loneliness had a purpose or positive aspect; perhaps it helped me to develop some inner awareness and thoughtfulness, although often self-indulgent, especially during adolescence!

After leaving school I worked as a trainee surveyor for a few years. When I turned twenty, I left home and went to University to study for a degree in Estate Management. During my second year at college, a series of stressful events (including nearly drowning, the end of a long-term relationship, the loss of a close friend, another close friend becoming very ill, and my own developing illness) lead to my having to leave college and return home, where my parents took on the task of looking after me. I had developed Post-Viral Syndrome (also known as Chronic Fatigue Syndrome, or CFS) after a bout of glandular fever. I could not do any of the basic household jobs like cooking, cleaning, or washing. I was so weak that I could not even hold my arms above my head to wash my own hair.

Over the next four years I spent most of my time either lying down or being pushed around in a wheelchair. I suffered bouts of clinical depression during this time and experienced other minor disasters: a serious car accident, a frightening near-death experience, the death of a well-loved pet, and a break-in and robbery at our home. I had come to expect problems and unhappiness as a normal part of living.

It is difficult to communicate the darkness and pain that often filled me and affected my family during those years. There were, however, some rare and golden moments. Perhaps difficult times strip away much of what we don't really need, open our minds, and make our awareness more acute. I can only say that there were windows in the darkness that suggested possibilities of something within myself beyond suffering; something so deep and wide and clear and pure that ordinary words or thoughts cannot touch.

Looking back on these difficult times and feeling as well and content as I do now, it almost seems like a different lifetime. Although I would not recommend illness as a way to self-awareness, I feel very fortunate to have experienced those difficulties, to have gained from them, and to have come out the other side a little wiser, stronger, and more aware.

Toward the end of another desperate winter and just before spring of 1993, a spiritual healer friend told me about Reiki and that an American Reiki Master would give a talk and teach Reiki locally. Although I'd tried many forms of complementary therapy, and although most had helped to relieve *some* of my symptoms, none had greatly improved my quality of life, which was really very low. I wasn't too excited about trying a new therapy. In fact, I think I only went to the talk because of my friend's enthusiasm.

From the moment I sat with the other people waiting to listen to the Reiki Master, I sensed something good was about to happen. There was something else that I couldn't put my finger on, something in the background, behind the good-natured chatter and smiling faces, some positive force that I knew and felt familiar with. At the time I could only describe it as a deeply nurturing, loving, and protective presence—now I also remember its presence during my very early childhood.

As soon as the Master was introduced to us, I felt what I can only describe as a "shift" or "movement within," as if something clicked into place. Perhaps it was the beginning of a deeper, inner connection to the presence that I first felt before the talk began. The rest of the evening was wonderful. It was fascinating to hear the story of Mikao Usui, the founder of Reiki, and amazing to feel Reiki for the first time. All my aches, pains, and stress fell away, and I left on a cloud of health and happiness.

Everyone at home was very pleased but perplexed to see how well I seemed. By the next day, the healthy feeling had partly worn off but it had left me with a new sense of hope that there was something that might help in some way. So I signed up for the First Degree Reiki course the following weekend, and hoped I would be well enough to attend.

In the days leading up to the course I had my doubts about Reiki. I didn't want to be disappointed again, but I kept reminding myself that if I didn't try it I might miss something special. Even before the course began, something seemed to already have changed for the better, as if a small flame had been lit within me, drawing me toward Reiki. I had great cause for optimism, an emotion I had been scared to feel for several years.

The weekend came for the First Degree course and although I did not feel well, I was determined not to miss out. By the time the class began, I was already feeling a little stronger. Nothing could have prepared me for First Degree Reiki. It was a complete revelation, a weekend that transformed my life. There was a special atmosphere of expectant optimism and friendship among the group, all of whom came from different backgrounds but somehow seemed already close. Many friendships were struck, and special experiences shared. The deeply loving presence that I had felt at the introductory talk seemed to surround each of us and my connection to it grow stronger over the two days. During the attunements it seemed so especially strong that Reiki almost took on a physical presence, like a gentle refreshing mist or light rain that helped to wash away all my physical and mental tension and illness.

Over the weekend course, I experienced waves of deep peace. When this happened, I just closed my eyes and allowed myself to open up, relax, and let go of a lot of inner junk that seemed to easily arise and dissipate as these waves of healing swept over me. Sometimes it felt as though my body and mind had become very light and was floating in this sense of deep peace and loving protection. One of the most remarkable things was that these experiences also felt perfectly normal and natural, as though I was *already* familiar with them.

The most uplifting aspect of the whole course was to actually feel the Reiki energy coming from my own hands after the first attunement, and also during my first self-treatment. Having felt the effects of Reiki previously, I knew that if I could give myself Reiki regularly, then my condition would definitely improve. Until I could actually feel Reiki coming from my own hands, I doubted that I might be able to channel Reiki as others did! This is a common (and completely unfounded) worry among new practitioners.

The first attunement was very special, I was a little excited and tried to calm myself. I thought that if I was tense, then the Reiki might not be able to enter my energy system. As soon as the lights were turned down and I closed my eyes, I felt my body automatically relax. All tension drained away and I felt light, peaceful, and a little sleepy. Although the Master's touch was very light, for a few moments my body felt as though it was being pushed down toward the floor from above. As the Master continued with the attunement, it seemed as though my energy system opened up from the top of my head down through the center of my body—as if I had a large, empty tube running from the crown of my head down to my base chakra. This tube filled with what I can only describe as "light energy" and the heavy feeling disappeared, leaving me feeling very happy, contented, and complete; a state I remained in for some time. When the Master touched my hands, I felt an increase in this light energy.

After the attunement we each shared our experiences—all of which were completely different! The Master then showed us how to feel the energy between our hands. This was for me a wonderfully empowering moment. After all my family and I had been through, and all the times I had to rely on others, I could now definitely help myself. I felt human again.

We then gave ourselves a first self-treatment, which was a very peaceful, healing, personal experience. Like the beginning of a new relationship, each of us was getting to know Reiki for ourselves rather than listening to others talk about it or receiving it through others.

It was also great to feel Reiki coming through when I gave my first Reiki treatment to someone else and afterwards to hear what they had experienced during that treatment. It still amazes me almost daily to feel Reiki present in my life and I still occasionally wonder if it will be there when I place my hands on someone. It always is! I must admit that there are times when I do take Reiki for granted, perhaps because it is such a constantly giving companion. When I remember how much help I have received, and continue to receive daily, I feel especially blessed.

After the First Degree course, I was strong enough to take a holiday, so I stayed at a friend's house in Kent for a few weeks while they were away. My health continued to improve and within a month I was completely able to look after myself—something I hadn't done for four years. It was like being reborn! The sense of freedom and newness of life, the possibilities of planning a future, and just enjoying the simple pleasures, like going for a walk, cooking a meal, or swimming, were astounding. The health improvements alone were wonderful.

However, the continuing experience of Reiki itself was even more special. It was as if with every self-treatment some precious part of my own being, my own center, was beginning to return. Something I had perhaps consciously and subconsciously been looking for since early childhood, but in all the wrong places! This experience of Reiki as a path toward inner and outer health, a process of opening the heart and mind and moving towards my own center, has stayed with me and has only deepened over time.

When I returned home from Kent, my mind turned to the possibility of Second Degree Reiki, although I did not have enough money to pay for it at the time. Our Master had taught us to set an intent using Reiki, and I trusted that if it was the right time, the money necessary would arrive. Sure enough it did!

Six months after taking First Degree Reiki, I took Second Degree Reiki and, again, nothing could have prepared me for it. I had been told a little of what to expect in terms of the use of symbols, but it really was a wonderful revelation to receive them and to be taught how to take a more active and responsible role in my experience of Reiki.

As with First Degree, I felt as though I had achieved something really worthwhile. Even though the Reiki courses are quite short and simple to complete, the sense of success and achievement was far greater than anything I had experienced in all my years of studying and taking exams at school, college, or university. I can only think that this was because receiving Reiki felt so meaningful to me as an individual. The four years of illness had in some way lead up to receiving Reiki, almost like another degree course in life—receiving Reiki was like my *real graduation!*

Finding My Spiritual Path

Shortly after finding Reiki, I met a friend who was also new to Reiki. We both became very interested in Buddhism, and eventually decided to live in a Buddhist residential center to see if it was right for us. Discovering Reiki and Buddhism together was a wonderful experience. We shared many special times and learned much about ourselves and the way of Reiki and Buddha.

I discovered that Buddhism provided me with an explanation of the experiences I received through Reiki. This increased understanding seemed to actually enhance the experiential Reiki path. It became less easy to see where Reiki ended and Buddhism began, and vice versa. For Reiki to appeal to people of all cultures and religions when it came to the West, it lost much of its Buddhist history, that is, the true Japanese account of Mikao Usui's story. Knowledge of this history is not necessary to use Reiki effectively, but I found that awareness of Buddha's conventional teachings greatly enriched my personal understanding and use of Reiki.

I learned two important things: what Reiki actually is, and how to use Reiki most effectively. I don't think any other spiritual path explains this with quite the same clarity and purpose. That is not to say that Buddhism is better than any other spiritual path, or that a Buddhist is a better Reiki practitioner. The teachings of all the great religions have many similarities, indeed some Christians, Muslims, or Jews are better Buddhists than some Buddhists, and vice versa! It all comes down to the individual and his or her relationship with herself, himself, God, Buddha, Allah, or whatever that person believes in. Buddhism works so well with Reiki because it is the "home" of Reiki; it is the spiritual context in which Reiki, as we know it today, came into this world. I think there is a lot we can learn from that. You do not have to be Buddhist to practice Reiki well, or to benefit from the Buddha's teachings—they are both open to everyone. Whatever your spiritual path, or path of personal growth, Reiki can enrich it and bring you closer to your full potential as a human being.

After taking Second Degree Reiki, my health continued to improve to the point where I was able to become self-employed and live without the physical or financial support of my parents. However, I think it is important to mention that shortly after becoming a Reiki Master in November, 1995, I had another bout of CFS. It took some time for me to understand why this relapse happened, since I'd expected my health to continue to improve after becoming a Master. It comes back to receiving what you need from life rather than what you want; certainly it was quite a humbling experience to be ill again and it made me look very closely at my approach to life. Perhaps I was trying to control things too much, trying to order and mold life to suit myself.

Learning to develop *the courage to let go* is a healthy part of living with Reiki. I don't think we can contain or control Reiki any more than we can contain or control the power of nature. To a certain extent, we have to learn to respect the fact that if we really want to benefit from Reiki, we have to try to leave behind that part of ourselves that is small and self-centered. Then Reiki can begin to bring out the best in us and help us learn to accept, adapt and rise to the changes and challenges that life brings.

The importance of allowing yourself to trust and be guided, moving on, not stagnating and trying not to manipulate life for your own benefit is paramount to a successful and swift journey. Honesty, openness, and courage lead to wisdom and inner strength. Reducing our selfishness and developing compassion or concern for others leads to the greatest happiness.

Becoming a Master was initially quite a sobering experience, not what I would have liked or expected if it had been my choice! What I have learned from this experience has added so much to my own understanding of Reiki that I can now see the value of that experience. Since recovering from the CFS relapse, the joy of being part of the process of introducing others to Reiki has more than made up for any discomfort or temporary disillusionment. To see how much other people benefit from Reiki has been wonderful to witness, a real privilege, and to see the changes that new practitioners experience even during one weekend is marvelous. To be part of that attunement process is always a very powerful, humbling, and healing experience.

Sometimes Reiki is presented in an overly "rosy, New Age" light, perhaps as an answer to all our problems. I know I am sometimes guilty of this. I can only say from my own short experience that Reiki may not be a cure-all for some people. Indeed, in some instances, it may seem that Reiki actually makes life *more* difficult as you become aware of areas of yourself that need to be acknowledged. Sometimes Reiki shows us our reflection very clearly, like an inner mirror, and this is not always what we would like to see. Although we all possess infinite potential, we are not perfect beings at present, and pretending that we are can prevent us experiencing the special transformational power of honesty.

I can say that Reiki has always provided me with the optimum conditions to realize and ripen my own potential. However, this has not always been obvious when faced with a difficult situation that I would normally have avoided or dealt with in a way that was solely for my own benefit. If you can see Reiki as a helpful tool for personal growth or spiritual development rather than an answer in itself, then you are on a path that will eventually reveal the true nature of Reiki as inseparable from your own pure inner nature.

My first experience healing others was very swift and simple. A Buddhist teacher friend gave a public talk on the benefits of meditation at a local community group. It was a very special evening, and the many people present listened intently to the story of the Buddha, how his teachings came to the West, and how they are relevant today. The teacher led a simple, guided meditation on developing compassion, and after a long "question-and-answer" session, everyone stayed to chat and have a cup of tea.

Another friend to whom I had taught Reiki introduced me to a woman I had noticed earlier in the evening. She had difficulty walking and sitting, it seemed she had lower back or hip problems. We chatted for some time, and it seemed right to offer her some Reiki. So we went to the back of the room where it was quieter and I placed my hands on her lower back while we continued to talk about Reiki. After about ten minutes, I finished and was a little disappointed because she felt no different. I mentioned that often healing continues after the actual treatment and that she might feel some relief the next day.

About a week later I bumped into the friend who had introduced me to the woman with the back problem. She was very excited to tell me that the woman had awoken the next day to no pain, and was able to walk as normal for the first time in years.

Often a healing such as this can take weeks or months, and sometimes the sufferer has to learn Reiki for him or herself to gain continuous relief. If all the right conditions are in place, whatever they may be, nothing will stop a complete healing with only a little Reiki and few expectations!

A Gift from a Friend

It was my friend Connie who introduced me to the woman with the back problem. I'd met Connie at an evening meditation group meeting about three years previous; she was not Buddhist, did not believe in God, and had no interest in spiritual matters. She had attended the meeting simply to enjoy the company and peace and relaxation that she gained from the meditations.

When I first met Connie, she was in her early sixties and had suffered from cancer for five or six years, at which time she had already outlived her doctor's suggested life expectancy and obviously had no intention of "checking out" just yet. She was a very bubbly, energetic, down-to-earth, kind, and warm-hearted person who had obviously been through many difficult times, not the least of which was her illness. Most of the people around her often forgot she was ill as she never brought attention to it, unless it would benefit others in some way to hear her story, and I think it often did.

I found Connie a very easy person to get along with. She had a wicked sense of humor, and would go out of her way to help others whenever she could. Perhaps because I only knew Connie as a friend, I rarely saw a less-attractive side to her nature, something I suspect with most of us is not that distant. The courageous and creative way with which I saw Connie live peacefully with her illness made a great impression on me.

I taught Connie and some of her friends First and Second Degree Reiki, waiting about three months between each course. Connie invited us to use her house for treatments, which was perfect, and she went out of her way to make us all at home. She even had a dining table the same shape and size as a therapy couch! These teaching sessions were very special to me as they were my first after becoming a Reiki teacher. I learned a lot in a short space of time, made a few mistakes and had plenty of laughs—something Connie always encouraged.

It was a special experience for me to learn First Degree Reiki and feel Reiki coming from my own hands for the first time. However, this was more than matched by the experience of bringing the beautiful attunement energy through for the first time and then seeing others' reactions as they felt Reiki coming through while first treating themselves, and then each other. Connie especially enjoyed receiving Reiki from others and seemed to soak it up like a sponge!

I saw Connie frequently for a few months after the Second Degree course and she always seemed well, but after a while we lost touch for about a year. I spoke to her in the summer of 1997, just before she was about to move. She was still well, but not looking forward to moving. Then, at the beginning of winter, 1997, another friend phoned to say that Connie was very ill with a sudden reoccurrence of the cancer, which had spread rapidly. I went to see Connie the next day and it was obvious from her condition that she was very ill. Her son told me that the hospital had discharged her so she could spend her last few weeks at home with her family.

I gave Connie regular Reiki treatments during the three weeks before she died. Without Reiki, I could not have coped seeing a friend die in this way. I always felt clear, strong, and very supported during these visits and felt very grateful to be able to help Connie in some way. I always looked forward to seeing her and to our Reiki sessions. When you give healing to others, you are in effect giving healing to a part of yourself. The more severe the illness, the deeper the self-healing you experience.

I certainly found this the case with Connie; we both benefited greatly from Reiki and at times it was difficult to see who was really giving and who was really receiving the healing! Connie always said she looked forward to the sessions, they relaxed her greatly, and as they progressed her mental strength and outlook improved continuously. She often fell into a deep sleep, and I have never been so deeply moved by the power, presence, and love of Reiki as I was during those times.

Before she died, Connie received an Advanced Reiki attunement. This was not my intention, or hers—it just happened. Although the Master usually plays a more active role in the attunement process, this was not the case with Connie's empowerment. She was very relaxed. I laid my hands on her head and the atmosphere in the room changed and became charged with the attunement energy and the relevant Reiki symbols. I began to feel very hot as I sometimes do before an attunement, then to my surprise and delight we both seemed to light up like light bulbs. It was a special experience for both of us. Three days later Connie died. About a week later, just before New Year's eve, I attended her packed funeral service, full of peace, happiness, love, and loss.

Although I miss Connie, learning to allow death to be a part of life helped me to help her. When she was dying, there were people around her who were naturally in great distress. However, I found that because Reiki supported me greatly and helped me to see the wider picture and because our Reiki sessions were so enjoyable, I actually looked forward to being with her and being part of her transition. If we could learn to accept death in the way we accept birth, dying would become less stressful, especially for the person who is dying. A peaceful death is a great gift.

Although, from a Buddhist perspective, we may not be able to stem the flow of ripening negative karma that is causing a serious illness to develop, we can do much to transform such situations into something very special and life-enhancing, even in the face of death. I certainly feel that Connie's treatment was a success because true success is simply *the greatest good,* whatever that may be in a particular situation. It may be a complete healing, it may be learning to live more positively and creatively with the limitations that an illness imposes, or it may be accepting and transforming death and "dying well."

One final thing I have to thank Connie for, which brings my own story up-to-date, is this book. The experience of teaching Connie and her friends Reiki made me realize that there is a lot to "take in" in just one weekend, especially if you are completely new to self-healing techniques. So following my first experience teaching Reiki, I decided to write a manual that I could give to others to take away with them after the course and refer back to when necessary. I also thought that much of what I was learning from Buddhism at the time would be very relevant to Reiki practitioners of any level.

Even though giving Reiki is a very simple thing to do when a treatment is successful, I always feel a great sense of achievement and again I think this is because sharing Reiki is such a uniquely personal and meaningful thing to do. I am often still amazed that it works at all! The two healing stories given above show how different Reiki treatments can be and how Reiki's natural healing intelligence is completely flexible and adapts to the needs of the recipient without the Reiki practitioner having to get overly involved if he or she doesn't need to. When long-term treatment is required, Reiki seems to support and guide both the recipient and the giver so that any relationship that develops is clear and healthy.

Living with Reiki is like developing a friendship. Like all good relationships that stand the test of time, it is an ongoing learning process. Like many practitioners, I initially had a honeymoon period of a few weeks. Then, when I gradually began to come back to Earth, I started to understand that all would not be easy or perfect unless I was prepared to learn the "way of Reiki." That is how to use Reiki in a way that is balanced and grounded in everyday life; in a way that is not selfish, but always serves the highest good for yourself and for others.

I am gradually discovering this principle through daily experience and studying Buddha's teachings. Reiki has not necessarily given me what I want, but has always given me what I *need*—often two very different things! The wisdom to understand this, the patience to accept it, and the wish to follow this path, is still for me in its infancy. It is a path worth walking, and though there are miracles, there are also no easy answers.

If you can open yourself to the possibilities of miracles, and yet live realistically, creatively, and positively within your limitations, you will have many wonderful experiences and develop special and lasting inner qualities. With a little wisdom and good will, Reiki can gradually lead you along this middle way toward your *own* center—the center of all things.

1

The Essence of Reiki

Reiki is the name given to a simple yet profound system of natural healing for body and mind, which was developed by Dr. Mikao Usui who lived in Japan during the nineteenth century. *Rei* means "universal," and *ki,* or *chi,* in Chinese, means "Life Force Energy." Many people also regard Reiki as a path to personal and spiritual growth.

Although most people cannot see chi. modern physics tells us that beyond the level of the smallest particles of matter, energy exists everywhere, in the air we breathe, in our food and water, and in light from the sun. Even inanimate objects possess a low or slow frequency of energy.

A Foundation of All Life

Life Force Energy is the foundation of all life, a sort of subtle cosmic soup that supports, nourishes, and sustains the cycle of birth, life, and death of all living things. When we are in touch with this energy through prayer, meditation, or Reiki, we feel less separate and increasingly whole within ourselves and within the whole of creation. We experience a sense of unity, we become more aware of our place or role in the great scheme of things and at the same time we feel supported, safe, open, and confident in our abilities to be all that we are, without doubt or apology. We can say that these spiritual or personal experiences are the Essence of Reiki as opposed to the Form that are the actual physical and mental methods for using and sharing Reiki.

From Buddhism and other Eastern spiritual traditions we understand that there are two main types of Life Force Energy: Internal and External. Internal Life Force Energy is the subtle energy that exists within the body and mind of all living beings. External Life Force Energy exists within plants, flowers, trees, rocks, minerals, and crystals, and this energy is often harnessed for healing purposes as in the Bach flower remedies, crystal healing, flower essences, homeopathic, and herbal remedies. Even just a walk in the countryside can have a calming and healing effect, as there is so much pure External Life Force Energy available that it lifts our own internal energies. This natural energy has a corresponding effect on our body and mind. Conversely, if we spend too much time in urbanized areas or stressful environments where these natural energies are restricted, this may adversely affect our health, especially if we are unable to mentally transcend or rise above these situations.

Internal Life Force Energy runs through subtle pathways or meridians in the human body. When these pathways are blocked or imbalanced, due to stress for example, illness can result. Most complementary therapies seek to help the body and mind rebalance and cleanse these internal energies, thereby promoting health and well-being. This is also the way Reiki works as a healing technique.

There are many levels of Internal and External Life Force Energy in the universe. On one level Reiki can be seen as the purest form of External Life Force Energy and it can have a profound effect on our health and well-being by re-balancing, cleansing, and renewing our Internal Energy System. When Reiki comes into contact with Internal Life Force Energy that is blocked, sluggish, or imbalanced, it naturally and effortlessly dissolves, transmutes, and raises the quality of that energy to the healthiest level that our body, mind, and environment will allow.

A Conscious Energy

When Internal and External Life Force Energy are in harmony, possess the same level of purity, and exist on the same wavelength or frequency, they are very similar energies. The only difference is that Internal Life Force Energy has consciousness or mind, and cannot exist separately from it.

Due to the close relationship between consciousness and Internal Life Force Energy it is easy to believe that the sense of closeness or companionship we feel towards trees, crystals, the Earth, or other sources of External Life Force Energy is because they possess a personal character or mind. External Life Force Energy, like that within trees, crystals, and the Earth does not possess consciousness or mind. This does not, however, make them any less special or sacred "living" objects.

Our internal energies and our mind are inseparable and have a very intimate dependent relationship. In fact, although we do not generally notice it, our thoughts and feelings "ride" on our internal energies. If we carry positive Internal Life Force Energy of a good quality, perhaps because it is enhanced with Reiki, it is easier for us to develop positive states of mind and we generally attract positive life experiences and deal with problems more easily. Likewise, if we consciously try to develop positive states of mind (like confidence, kindness, and wisdom) this will raise the quality of our internal energies and in turn improve our health and many other aspects of our lives. With a good motivation, Reiki can greatly assist us in improving our quality of life, helping us become more whole and healthy beings on all levels and therefore naturally benefitting those around us.

Hawayo Takata, who some traditional Western Reiki practitioners regard as the Third Reiki Grand Master, explained it in a 1970s Hawaii newspaper article this way: "Here is the great space, which surrounds us, the Universe. There is endless and enormous energy. It is universal. Its ultimate source is the creator. It is a limitless force. It is the source of energy that makes plants grow and birds fly. When a human being has pain or problems, he or she can draw from it. It is an external source, a wavelength of great power, which can revitalize and restore harmony. It is nature. It is God. The power he makes available to his children who seek it."

More Than Just Energy

Many Reiki practitioners from both religious and nonreligious backgrounds have noticed their spiritual lives renewed or reborn as a result of Reiki, almost as if Reiki has the ability to lead people, if they wish, to a deeper awareness of their own spirituality or potential for personal growth.

So it would seem there are many facets to Reiki, it is not just an Energy. In fact, this suggests that Reiki possesses wisdom and compassion or that Reiki is an expression of a level of consciousness whose essence is complete wisdom and compassion. If we know that consciousness rides on Internal Life Force Energy, then perhaps we can see Reiki as the Universal Internal Life Force Energy of the most open, advanced, expanded, and pure form of consciousness. Reiki may just presently appear to us as an external energy because of our current lack of deep insight and our limited awareness.

Pure Wind from a Pure Land

Many Buddhist texts refer to Life Force Energy as Subtle Wind and this is a good description of how many people experience Reiki. So we could refer to Reiki as a Pure Subtle Wind or blessing coming from a special place, perhaps Pure Wind from a Pure Land. "Pure Land" is the Buddhist phrase for heaven; an outward manifestation of the mind of enlightenment.

As limited beings we live in a world of conflicting conceptual dualities: good and bad, light and dark, internal and external, have and have not, self and other. The essence of Reiki seems to transcend and go beyond the duality of an internal or external world towards a balanced completeness, unity, and wholeness, where there are no limitations of identity or barriers between self and other. Ultimately, Reiki is inexpressible or indescribable, only experiential, boundless loving kindness, wisdom, beauty, and perfection.

The Awakened One

Many spiritual traditions honor the idea of "Full Enlightenment." In fact, the word "Buddha" means "Awakened One." The mind of enlightenment is omniscient; it pervades the whole of space and time and perceives the true nature of all phenomena directly and simultaneously. It is the synthesis of the greatest peace, joy, love, compassion, and wisdom.

Buddha's main purpose is to prevent or relieve suffering and bring all living beings to the same state of complete consciousness or wholeness, if that is what they wish. Many followers of other religions would also equate these ideas with their own perception or experience of God. Perhaps, then, the gift of Reiki as a healing technique is simply an expression or emanation of loving kindness: a form of blessing, empowerment, and connection to a higher source that is close to our own true nature, and that has our own best intentions at heart.

Confining Reiki to a convenient definition is difficult and has only a limited value. When we experience Reiki, it appears to come from an *external* source. Whether we believe that it comes from an external creator, or is a reflection of our own higher nature or greatest potential is not important. There are no belief systems or dogma attached to Reiki. It is taught and practiced in almost every country of the world. Its peaceful, healing intelligence extends beyond religious, cultural, and political boundaries. Reiki is an experiential phenomena, uniquely personal, yet completely universal.

One Path, But Not The Only Path

Reiki fits perfectly into any lifestyle materially, mentally, emotionally, and spiritually. Reiki gives us exactly what we need as individuals, helping us develop our unique qualities, talents and ambitions in a way that brings us closer to our own limitless potential and inner nature, the bond we share with all living beings. Any explanation of what Reiki is or what it can do is merely scratching the surface.

The true essence of Reiki goes beyond concepts, words, and ideas. However, we do need words and ideas or "form" to teach, communicate, and share Reiki with others. In this sense, the Traditional Form, as taught by Reiki Masters since Dr. Usui's time, is an important gateway to the essence. We need to discuss and share our Reiki experiences in order to gain mental clarity of their meaning, to digest and integrate these insights within our being, to enable us to move forward and enrich our daily lives. So we also need form in the aspect of conceptual thoughts and language to enable us to open our hearts and minds and gradually learn our lessons.

For some people Reiki is simply a useful healing technique. For others it may be a complement to their current spiritual path or actually a path to spiritual and personal growth in itself. According to the way we view the world, each of us will have a different opinion and experience of Reiki. However, we all share the same basic wish to be happy and the same opportunity to benefit from Reiki, so in this sense we are of one mind.

We all carry within us the ability to heal ourselves and others. Some people can access this quite easily through prayer or meditation without Reiki. Reiki is not essential in order to develop an ability to heal or to advance along a spiritual path, but it can greatly assist.

2

The Story of Reiki

Healing systems similar to Reiki are referred to in many ancient religious scriptures. However, we can be sure that the origins of Reiki go back far beyond recorded history. As many of the great cultures died out, their knowledge of healing techniques was also lost, diluted, or absorbed by other traditions. Whenever there has been a great need for a simple and effective healing system for body, mind, and spirit, Reiki has arisen in one form or another.

Since Reiki first came to the West from Japan, the traditional "Story of Reiki" has become a well loved and integral part of the teaching practice of many Reiki Masters. Almost every Reiki practitioner is told this story, and until quite recently no one questioned its authenticity. Most Western Reiki Masters trace their lineage back to Hawayo Takata. She is recognized by many in the West as the Third Reiki Grand Master, and as you will see later, the one who brought Reiki out of Japan. At some point during this transition the original Story of Reiki was adapted, probably with good intentions, to be more acceptable or perhaps more easily understood by Westerners.

When the story of Reiki was first told in the West it would have seemed very strange and perhaps almost pagan without the Christian aspect which may have been introduced by Hawayo Takata or her Master Dr. Chujiro Hayashi. Also postwar America would not have been in a pro-Japanese frame of mind and consequently not very receptive to Reiki as a Japanese, non-Christian healing technique. Whoever decided to do this and for whatever reason it might have been a very wise and brave decision. They must have realized that one day, perhaps when the time was right, the more accurate story would become widely known and by that time the adapted story would have served its purpose by making Reiki easily acceptable and so more widespread. If we see the main purpose of Reiki as relieving suffering and improving quality of life, then the more people that benefit from it the better. So in this sense adapting the original story may have been a wise decision which has now served its purpose.

Western Reiki practitioners face a transition toward a clearer awareness of our roots. A few Reiki Masters have in recent years worked hard to discover a more accurate story of Reiki. Although this research is by no means complete, we are beginning to build up a picture from their work. It points to a fascinating, more complete, and clearer version of the events surrounding the life of Mikao Usui and how Reiki is taught in Japan today, as he originally taught it.

Both the traditional Western story and a more concise version of the most recent research are presented in this chapter. It seems that new information regarding Mikao Usui and "Japanese Reiki" is constantly coming to light and this is likely to continue for some time. If you want to become aware of this information as soon as it is made widely available, you will need to access the Internet. There are some excellent articles and much interesting information on many aspects of Reiki on the World Wide Web.

Figure 2.1 Reiki Founder Dr. Mikao Usui
(Used with kind permission of Phyllis Lei Furumoto)

There are many aspects of the traditional story of Reiki that are not recognized or verified in Japan. However, the traditional story is still relevant and a unique part of our Reiki culture and heritage. It will no doubt continue to be told in one form or another for many years. It is, in essence, very close to the original Japanese version, and has a special "energy" when it is told as part of a public talk, or during a First Degree Reiki class. Close to the heart of Reiki, it certainly communicates many valuable insights into the practice and understanding of Reiki. For this reason it may stand the test of time alongside the new information we will receive from Japan.

The Traditional Story

Not so long ago there lived a man who had a burning question: "How did Jesus heal?" Could those people who were following a similar path of spiritual development as Jesus also heal as he had done? In short, was it true what Jesus had said: "All these things that I have done you can do, and yet greater things." The story of this quest has been passed down from master to student in its original form since Reiki was first taught. A personal understanding of this modern parable, which contains many lessons about human nature, healing, and wholeness, has always been encouraged and is central to the successful use and practice of Reiki as we know it today.

Dr. Mikao Usui was born in 1864 in Japan and was raised by Christian missionaries. While most Japanese children were brought up under the traditional Shinto and Buddhism religions, Mikao Usui studied the Bible and the stories and teachings of Jesus. After leaving school and choosing to study religion, he became a professor of theology and was eventually appointed the head and minister of a Christian Boys' School.

One morning, while conducting a chapel service, he was questioned by several of the senior boys on his beliefs. They asked if he literally believed in the biblical miracles Jesus had performed. He replied that he did. They then asked him to demonstrate his faith by performing a miracle! He was speechless and found it incredible that such a simple question should shake his faith so completely. Deeply affected by this incident, he felt he could not honestly continue to teach about the life and example of Jesus. He decided to resign, and dedicate the rest of his life to deepening his faith and discovering how such healing miracles could be performed. Deep within he knew that if his faith was true, he would be able to receive the gift of healing and help many others do the same. He knew that if he did not follow this calling he would deeply regret it later in life.

A Search for Christ

Christianity was not widespread in Japan, so Dr. Usui emigrated to America, where he spent many years studying the Christian scriptures more closely. He explored his questions with many scholars and members of the church. Many times he was disheartened and discouraged by their answers, and he often felt no closer to finding the truth. Yet he developed great inner resources and came to rely less upon those he met for answers and more upon his own deepening relationship with God and upon his own natural, intuitive wisdom. During his search, he experienced many coincidences and often felt guided—and sometimes almost pushed—into situations that held clues and signals toward the next step of his journey. These occurrences (such as chance meetings with others on similar spiritual paths and the subsequent insights they gave him) encouraged and deepened his faith and allowed him to trust that he would be shown, or that he would "know" where to look next.

Dr. Usui also studied the writings and teachings of many other famous spiritual teachers and mystics, not exclusively from the Christian tradition. He felt that this would complement and enrich his own faith and understanding of the spiritual path and his search for the gift of healing. He often studied the teachings of Buddha and the accounts of his disciples and their healing ministry, which seemed to him very similar to those of Jesus and his own followers. As he discovered more similarities between the Buddhist and Christian paths he gradually realized from within himself that the final answers to his questions might lie much closer to home!

After seven years in America, Dr. Usui returned to Kyoto, Japan, to study the Buddhist sutras, the records of Buddha's life and teachings, in more depth. He visited many Buddhist centers, however he found that the Buddhist monks and nuns, like the Christian missionaries, mainly taught and encouraged spiritual growth and the practice of healing was considered a distraction to that growth. The main purpose of their mission was to help people achieve inner happiness in spite of external problems like illness or poverty, which people cannot avoid sooner or later. Healing was left to the practices of conventional and complementary medicine.

Finding a Buddha

During his studies and travels throughout Japan, Dr. Usui met a Zen Buddhist abbot who was to have a profound effect on him and his spiritual journey. The abbot invited

Dr. Usui to live and study at his monastery, and for several years Dr. Usui remained there. The calm, clear, and tranquil environment of the monastery gave him the perfect space to assess the work he had done in America and during his stay he became more and more convinced that the only place to look for the ability to heal was within himself.

The abbot was a great inspiration to him and they spent many hours discussing his progress and how best to achieve his goals. His relationship with the abbot developed and Dr. Usui came to recognize him as a great yet very humble man with a boundless source of wisdom and compassion. The abbot became Dr. Usui's spiritual guide along the inner path towards the source of his own being. Dr. Usui's own inner healing or the unfolding or blossoming of his own consciousness would bring him within reach of the gift of healing.

Studying the Sutras

Dr. Usui studied and meditated on the Buddhist scriptures, or sutras, in Japanese, Chinese, and Sanskrit (one of the oldest and most sublime spiritual languages, which Buddha Shakyamuni himself spoke and taught over 2,000 years ago). Within the ancient Sanskrit texts, he discovered the symbols that would lead him, through prayer and meditation, to the healing techniques he was searching for. At first he did not know exactly what to do with the symbols or how to use them as tools for healing.

As his studies progressed, he found passages in the sutras that seemed to stand out or "speak" to him and he read and meditated frequently on these same teachings, each time gaining deeper meaning. He often discussed his thoughts with the other monks and the abbot, always trying to steadily further his awareness. This dedication steadily enabled him to unfold and expand his own consciousness so that he could gain clear insights into the nature of the mind and how it not only had the power to create, but also heal physical, emotional, and mental illness. He became even more aware of others' suffering and this deep empathy added greater determination to his efforts.

Retreat to the Mountain

Dr. Usui knew he had studied all he could and that the answers he sought were finally within his reach. He went to a sacred Buddhist mountain retreat near Kyoto that had an especially pure level of Life Force Energy. There he fasted and meditated for three weeks, cleansing the remaining obstructions within his own mind and opening himself up completely to whatever he might be ready to receive. He told the abbot at the monastery that if he did not return after twenty-one days, they should come to collect his remains for burial. He was so focused on his mission and motivated by the wish to benefit others that he did not intend to return without an answer to all his questions.

Walking the seventeen miles to the mountain, he found a quiet place by a stream. He intended to only drink water during his retreat, which he knew from experience would give more clarity and power to his meditations. He kept with him twenty-one stones, and each day he cast one away to mark the passing of time. He meditated upon the lessons he learned at the monastery under the guidance of the abbot. His concentration was very strong and stable and his internal energies so clear that he was easily able to continually manifest or experience the purity of his own inner light or very subtle mind. When this very high level of consciousness is completely purified, it becomes the omniscient mind of a Buddha, or perhaps from another perspective creates a complete union with God or Christ-Consciousness.

An End, and a Beginning

One morning, Dr. Usui found he had only one stone left. It was the final day of his retreat. He meditated in the darkness that preceded the first light of dawn and experienced many mixed emotions and recollections of his life. He knew that his quest was ending and that soon his life would be over or he would be given the gift of healing to share with others. His faith and devotion were complete, he had done all that he could and now he knew he had reached the point of no return.

Looking into the darkness, he saw a light on the horizon where he expected to see the sun rise. It grew brighter and brighter, and appeared to move toward him very fast. He realized that if he did not move, it would hit him. He was determined to relax, open, and allow this experience to happen wherever it might lead. He centered himself and remained where he was, knowing that this would be an end and a beginning. The light struck his forehead and he lost consciousness.

Clear Light Consciousness

When Dr. Usui awoke, it was midday. He remembered everything that had happened. After the light had struck him, he became aware of beautiful colors and sensations, followed by a great light filling the whole of space—the nature of pure wisdom, compassion, and bliss. Within this light, large transparent bubbles appeared, each containing the Sanskrit symbols he had found in the Buddhist texts. As he memorized the contents of each bubble, it moved away and the next one would appear. His body, speech, and mind were fully empowered with the Reiki energy and symbols, and he understood the complete meaning of each symbol.

This knowledge arose spontaneously, almost as if the giver and receiver were of the same nature. It seemed as though he had only temporarily forgotten this inner truth, and he now remembered or recalled this knowledge from deep within himself. He called it Reiki, or Universal Life Force Energy.

Four Reiki Miracles

Dr. Usui felt deeply touched, privileged, and excited by what had happened, and wanted to return quickly to the monastery to share his experiences with the abbot, who had given him so much and been so instrumental in his search to discover Reiki.

In his rush to return to the monastery and tell the abbot of his discovery, Dr. Usui stubbed his toe on a rock. His toe painfully bleeding, he quickly sat and held the foot between his hands. The wound healed instantly. This was the first Reiki healing miracle.

On his journey back, he stopped at a roadside cafe and ordered a large meal. At first the cook refused to serve him, noticing that the doctor had just returned from a long fast and declaring that such a meal would make him very ill. But Dr. Usui insisted, and subsequently felt no ill effect. This was the second Reiki miracle. The meal was brought by the cook's granddaughter, who was in much pain with an infected tooth. Dr. Usui asked if he could touch the swollen area and the pain stopped and the swelling immediately went down. This was the third healing miracle. Dr. Usui was elated and continued his journey to the monastery to share his good news.

At the monastery, the monks told Dr. Usui that the abbot was confined to his room suffering from arthritis. Dr. Usui bathed and dressed in clean clothes and visited the abbot who was very pleased to see him and to hear about his discovery. The abbot asked for a demonstration, which immediately relieved his condition. They discussed how Dr. Usui could use his healing gift and which people where most in need of Reiki.

Dr. Usui decided to live in the slums of Kyoto where he would offer Reiki to the poor and homeless. Then when they were ready he would help them find jobs and send some of the younger ones to the monastery, where they would be trained by the monks in skills to support themselves. The abbot was very supportive of Dr. Usui's intentions but reminded him, "You must heal the whole person, a temporary healing of body and mind is not enough, people have to be genuinely seeking long-term positive change within themselves before a permanent healing is possible."

A Valuable Lesson

Dr. Usui spent a number of years practicing and teaching Reiki in the poorest areas of Kyoto and, although his intentions and offers of help often met with derision, he did not give up as many people seemed to be benefiting from Reiki. However, after some time he began to notice some of his earlier Reiki students begging on the streets again and he asked them why they were doing this. They told him that working and earning a living was much harder than going out to beg each day. Even though they had been able to support themselves they lacked the effort or wish to continue improving or maintaining their position.

On discovering this, Dr. Usui was very disheartened. He gave up his mission and withdrew to meditate on what had happened. He thought of the monks and the emphasis they placed on encouraging moral discipline, self-development and spiritual ethics, and he realized that it was this aspect of his healing ministry with the beggars that was lacking. It seemed that Reiki had helped them to see that a different way of life was possible and had initially supported and enabled positive physical and mental changes. However, their wish for permanent change was weak and not based on a strong continuous intention to improve themselves or an understanding of the danger of the downward spiral they were on physically, mentally, and spiritually.

Consequently the momentum of their improved morality and attitudes slowed and they were drawn back by the weight of their old, deeply ingrained habits. This was not a judgement of how all the beggars should have lived, for we all have the right to determine our own path in life and indeed many of those early patients, who sincerely tried, were able to transform their lives permanently with the help of Reiki. So Dr. Usui had to completely review his approach to sharing Reiki with others and, after further contemplation and meditation, he introduced the Five Reiki Principles as a daily part of Reiki practice:

Just for today do not worry.
Just for today do not anger.
Honor your parents, teachers, and elders.
Earn your living honestly.
Show gratitude to every living thing.

These are the principles as taught by many Western Reiki Masters, and are very similar to the Japanese version, originally attributed to the Meiji Emperor of Japan (1868–1912). In Dr. Usui's memorial inscription they are called The Five Principles of the Meiji Emperor (see Usui memorial on pages 34–37).

A Lantern in the Dark

Dr. Usui realized that, on the whole, he had to look for people with a real wish to improve their inner qualities as well as their quality of life. He decided to travel throughout Japan teaching Reiki wherever people were trying to create a better life and looking for an opportunity to learn and grow.

On reaching a town, he would often walk around in the daylight hours carrying a lighted lantern. People would laugh at him and ask why he carried the light. Having gained their attention, he would say, "All I see here is darkness, if you want to learn more about your own inner light you should come to my talk and demonstration this evening." There he would tell the story of Reiki and give healing to others and this is how many people came to Reiki in Japan.

Reiki Comes to the West

In the mid 1920s, Dr. Usui met Dr. Chujiro Hayashi, a forty-seven-year old naval reserve officer. Dr. Hayashi had spent most of his working life in the armed forces but had long held an interest in the spiritual path and the healing arts. Dr. Hayashi must have been deeply touched and impressed by Dr. Usui's peaceful yet powerful presence, his deep wisdom, and genuine compassion. After practicing and experiencing Reiki for some time under the guidance of Dr. Usui, he decided to devote the rest of his life to practicing and teaching Reiki.

It is said that Dr. Usui and Dr. Hayashi worked closely together to develop the actual "Form of Reiki," that is, how best to give treatments, the twelve hand positions, the different degrees of training, and how to teach Reiki. Dr. Hayashi's legacy and gift to us is a system of healing that has great clarity, strength, and simplicity, and which enables us to keep Reiki true to the Essence of Dr. Usui's intention. This combination of Essence and Form creates a clear lineage of how to practice and teach Reiki, so that practitioners many centuries into the future will be able to experience the Essence of Reiki and practice the Form as it was given to others many years ago. As more people become attuned to Reiki, the whole planet will benefit; deeper and clearer levels of consciousness and understanding will naturally arise in the minds of those seeking a lasting solution to global and personal problems but this continuity of global healing will only be possible if we can keep the Form of Reiki close to Dr. Usui's intention.

Following the death of Dr. Usui, Dr. Hayashi is said to have become the Second Reiki Grand Master. Dr. Usui was buried in a temple near Kyoto with the story of his life written on a memorial stone (see the translation at the end of this chapter). It is said that the grave was honored by the Emperor of Japan.

A New Era for Reiki

Dr. Hayashi ran a very successful Reiki clinic in Tokyo with other practitioners until 1940. During this time he taught and gave Reiki to many people, and kept detailed records of all his cases. Toward the end of the 1930s, Dr. Hayashi had a series of insights and intuitions regarding the imminent world war and how it would affect both himself and the future of Reiki. Because of his previous military experience, he could not avoid military service. Unable to reconcile his life as a healer with the possibility of harming others, and understanding that the potential war made the future of Reiki uncertain in Japan, he chose to confer Grand Master on someone who could continue his work elsewhere. He chose Mrs. Hawayo Takata to be the Third Reiki Grand Master. Mrs. Takata was an experienced and well-respected Reiki Master practicing in Hawaii and, as far as we know, she was the first person to take Reiki beyond the shores of Japan—a choice that symbolized Dr. Hayashi's trust and confidence in her.

Toward the end of his life, Dr. Hayashi taught Mrs. Takata all he had learned from Dr. Usui, and from his own experience. On the day he died, he summoned his close family, said his goodbyes and left them with special personal messages. He sat down in the traditional Japanese posture, meditated, and prayed for a short time. He then breathed a deep sigh and peacefully died. Dr. Hayashi, like his own Master Dr. Usui, was a great man. Together they were responsible for the creation and expansion of one of the most simple, profound, and complete healing systems we have ever known.

The Story of Mrs. Takata

Hawayo Takata was born in Hawaii in 1900, the American daughter of Japanese parents. When she was twenty-nine years old, her husband died and she was left without money to bring up her two small daughters. At thirty-five years old, she had serious health problems, she had lost a lot of weight and was severely distressed after the death of several family members. In the autumn of 1935, after she had almost come to the end of her endurance and following much prayer and soul searching, she had a clear intuition that an answer to her problems would be found in Japan.

Desperate, yet confident that her intuition came from God, she traveled to Tokyo to see a doctor friend at a hospital there. After many tests, she was told her only hope was surgery. She had another clear intuition prior to the operation that it would not be necessary, and that another form of treatment would become known to her. At the consternation of the doctors and nurses she refused the anesthetic and left her bed. While leaving the hospital, she asked her doctor friend if he was aware of any other treatment, and he told her of Dr. Hayashi's Reiki clinic. She visited Dr. Hayashi and, despite her initial skepticism of Reiki's simple, hands-on style, decided to continue regular treatments with him. To her surprise and delight, her health began to improve and this continued until all her problems had ceased.

Reiki Beyond Japan

Mrs. Takata's life was so completely and wonderfully transformed by Reiki that in her gratitude she needed to learn Reiki and share it with others. She asked Dr. Hayashi if he would teach her Reiki so she could practice it in Hawaii. Reiki had not been practiced outside of Japan, and Dr. Hayashi may have wondered if it would remain true to Dr. Usui's intention when interpreted by a different culture.

However, even at this stage, he must have realized that Reiki was destined to spread much further than Japan, so he agreed to Mrs. Takata's request on the condition that she remain in Japan as an apprentice practitioner for one year. During her apprenticeship she learned how to treat herself, how to give Reiki to others, and how to develop a deep personal relationship with Reiki so that in time she would need less guidance from Dr. Hayashi and be more able to rely on her own wisdom, intuition, and experience. Dr. Hayashi was very pleased with her progress during her training, and just before she returned to Hawaii, he initiated her into Second Degree Reiki.

Toward Becoming Master

After Mrs. Takata had successfully established a Reiki practice in Hawaii for two years, she invited Dr. Hayashi to visit in early 1938. He was very impressed with what she had achieved and how she had respected and emphasized the lineage and cultural tradition of Reiki. During this visit, Mrs. Takata was initiated as a Reiki Master.

Dr. Hayashi recognized Mrs. Takata's natural understanding and empathy toward the suffering of others resulted from her own difficult life experiences. Over the following years he also recognized her qualities of professional integrity, honesty, and appreciation for the value and potential of Reiki as a healing technique and as a tool for spiritual and personal growth. Often he felt that Hawayo Takata would be the ideal person to protect and carry on the Reiki lineage.

In 1941, not long before his death, although he had taught other masters, he decided that because of her complete dedication and great example of "living" Reiki, Mrs. Takata should succeed him as the Third Reiki Grand Master. Following Dr. Hayashi's death, she continued to practice and teach Reiki in Hawaii for many years, only teaching Reiki Masters in her seventies, when she felt certain her students were ready to receive, and that she and Reiki were ready to give.

The Fourth Western Reiki Grand Master

Hawayo Takata died on December 11, 1980, after having taught twenty-two Masters in the United States and Canada. Her granddaughter, Phyllis Lei Furumoto, became the Fourth Reiki Grand Master and holds this title today. When Phyllis was a little girl she recalled helping her grandmother give Reiki treatments, and Reiki being a natural part of everyday life. In a sense, this early bonding with Mrs. Takata was the beginning of her journey and apprenticeship toward one day becoming Grand Master herself. As she grew up, Reiki became less of an obvious presence in her life and she led a normal personal and professional life. Although Mrs. Takata often talked about her work with Reiki, it was not until Phyllis reached her early thirties that she considered her grandmother's requests to travel and practice Reiki with her.

The decision to do this was a turning point in Phyllis' life. They spent much time together as colleagues, practicing, talking, and arguing about Reiki! They sometimes differed in their approach to life and their work with Reiki. This relationship and process of learning from each other even continued for some time after Mrs. Takata's death, as Phyllis often felt her strong and peaceful presence. Their differences and discussions as Reiki Masters were a source of insight and self-discovery and perhaps served to give Phyllis confidence in her own ideas of how she wished to be as a Reiki Master, and finally as Grand Master.

A Global Reiki Community

Global awareness of Reiki has arisen by word of mouth, born from the positive experiences of individuals—a very organic and natural growth process. It was Mrs. Takata's wish that Reiki should become a well-known and respected form of healing throughout the world. The fulfillment of this wish has to some extent reshaped the role of Grand Master. Today the Western Grand Master is less of a spiritual figurehead with sole responsibility for the preservation of the lineage, and more of a facilitator who, by example, can enable and encourage individual practitioners, groups, and the wider Reiki community to find, develop, and establish their own natural processes of growth and order.

In more recent years, as Reiki has become popular all over the world, Phyllis has shared her responsibilities and the demands on her time with Paul Mitchell. Also a student of Mrs. Takata and a well-known and respected Reiki Master, Paul has great experience and a natural ability to express and communicate the Form of Traditional Reiki from the Western perspective. This increased emphasis on Form has arisen in response to the number and diversity of peoples and cultures now practicing Reiki and to the possibility that in time, without Form, we may somehow dilute or lose the ability to value, reach, and receive the Essence of Reiki.

Perhaps we can see Reiki as a tree with Form representing the branches and Essence as the sap; both mutually supportive and dependent for continuous healthy growth. To keep and protect the ability to reach the Essence of Reiki purely, the simple Form gives us a common guide or framework on a conscious level that Reiki teachers can communicate to their students in a similar way. Reiki seems to actually *encourage* individual and cultural differences of expression and creation while the Essence of these experiences stays timeless, universal, and common to all.

Together Phyllis and Paul complement and support each other, traveling as a team and as individuals, sharing their knowledge and example of living Reiki and helping to establish groups of Masters able to carry and communicate the Essence and Form of Reiki within their own particular communities and cultures. Perhaps this process is the way forward for Reiki and Reiki practitioners. Perhaps in a sense we can become our own Grand Masters. This process of self-empowerment seems to be the message that Phyllis and Paul are giving through their work.

Japanese Reiki: A New Beginning

Many aspects of the traditional Western story of Reiki have been brought into question and the new information in recent years regarding the origins of Reiki as known and practiced in Japan has been a breath of fresh air in the global Reiki community. It almost seems like we have opened the windows and allowed fresh energy to come in and take us to a new level of awareness. Such changes often bring minor conflict or differences of opinion, but this can only be positive if we are open to new ideas and inner growth. Perhaps the unveiling of this new information is symbolic of an opportunity for us to see ourselves, and Reiki, in a new light.

The following is an article by Frank Arjava Petter, well known for his work in discovering and presenting information regarding the roots of Reiki and how it is practiced in Japan today. The views he expresses offer us a different and perhaps clearer perspective about the lineage of Reiki in the West.

Reiki: Who Is In Charge?

by Frank Arjava Petter

I have had the opportunity to live in Japan and teach Reiki classes here since 1993. With the help of my Japanese wife, Chetna, and Shizuko Akimoto, a Japanese Reiki Master, I have had contact with several people who learned Reiki from Dr. Usui's early students as well as members of Dr. Usui's family and members of the Usui Shiki Ryoho of Tokyo. During these meetings we discussed the history of Reiki and how it is practiced in Japan. Through the benefit of these sources, I have learned many interesting things about Reiki that have not been known in the West.

For many years we all have been looking at Reiki history from a Western point of view. This story has had some limitations, and because of cultural and language barriers between Japan and the West, not many of the ideas in the Western story were able to be verified or explored. The life of Dr. Usui or Usui Sensei as he is called by his followers in Japan was one clouded in mists of a mystical character. Because of this, some misinformation about Usui Sensei and his life has developed. Recently the question of who the true successor of Usui Sensei is has come up again, and for that reason I would like to make things clear once and for all.

Since Usui Sensei died on March 9, 1926, the Usui Shiki Ryoho, which he founded and presided over, has had five sequential presidents, the true and only successors of Mikao Usui. The first successor was Mr. Ushida, who took over the responsibilities after Usui Sensei's death. The second successor was Mr. Iichi Taketomi, the third Mr. Yoshiharu Watanabe, the fourth Mr. Wanami, and the present successor is Ms. Kimiko Koyama.

The titles Grandmaster or Lineage Bearer were not and are not in use in the Usui Shiki Ryoho or Usui Kai as it is now called. Consequently this title was never passed on to Mr. Chujiro Hayashi as is currently believed in the West. The only successor to Usui Sensei was Mr. Ushida in 1926. Mr. Hayashi was one of many respected disciples of Usui Sensei, but not more and not less than that. In the old days disciples like Mr. Hayashi who were granted the teacher status by the president often had their own disciples. This is why there are so many different Reiki streams flowing all over Japan. However, there is no question about Ms. Kimiko Koyama's leadership today.

The reason that the truth about the real successor of Usui Sensei never came to the light in the West is rather simple. Years ago we heard on the phone from an Usui Kai member that they were not interested in Reiki that comes from a foreign country. This attitude explains why the record was never officially set straight. Japanese people in general are very accepting, much more so than Westerners. When it rains, it rains, and when the sun shines, the sun shines. Regarding things that are happening abroad, the Japanese interest is usually nil. This goes for environmental destruction, international wars, politics, and, of course, Reiki and the untruths that are circulated about it. So much abuse has been perpetrated in the name of Reiki that it is hardly surprising that the Japanese Usui Kai keeps its knowledge to itself. They just don't want to be involved.

However, I am neither Japanese nor of passive character and I have a passion for the truth. That is why I would like to leave the above information with all of you. Reiki is pure energy no matter what label we put on it. There is neither a right nor a wrong Reiki. Energy does not have moral attributes and can never be owned by anyone. It is our human birthright and therefore free as the wind.

In this spirit of love, light, and oneness I wish you all the best on your path to the light, from Japan with love.

Frank Arjava Petter is a Reiki Master living in Japan and the author of *Reiki Fire,* published by Lotus Light Publications.

Where to Next?

Petter's article gives an account of the type of new information that is coming to light regarding the roots of Reiki. His thoughts and observations serve to highlight the depth of passion that many practitioners feel regarding the future of Reiki and how we approach the subjects of lineage, form, and purity of practice. Clearer information regarding the history of Reiki will be invaluable in helping us to align ourselves with Dr. Usui's intentions and the essence of Reiki. However, many of the answers to these questions lie with the individual practitioner because ultimately they are personal challenges and therefore opportunities for personal growth.

The following article by Mary Ellis, an English Independent Reiki Master, looks at this more closely.

Reiki Integrity: Are We Reiki?

by Mary Ellis

The current confusion and cross-fire, in some cases involving lawsuits between Masters, has highlighted a time of profound, and at times painful, re-evaluation of my own learning and evolving through experiencing Reiki.

I found Reiki in 1992. I went to an introductory talk and during the evening we laid our hands on our heart chakras, and it was as though I had come home. I knew that whatever Reiki was it was right for me, and at a deeper, intuitive understanding I knew that ultimately Reiki was all we would ever need to heal ourselves and others, by allowing Reiki to flow through us.

Reiki is Love. More than the outward, visible hands-on healing it is the essence of unconditional love. If we were able to be this love, give it to others and ourselves, there would be no need for Reiki or any kind of healing because there would be no illness, no fear, anger, greed, sorrow, terror, pain, and despair, because love is the absence of all these.

I can recall the gradual steps of my awakening over the past five years, the subtle and steady change of someone who, because of fear, was constantly pushing, shoving and at times bullying others, to make happen what I wanted to happen. I was so desperate to get what I thought I needed to find fulfillment, happiness, security, peace, and love. I remember with deep gratitude the leaps in consciousness.

So what of this time of great confusion, of explosive cut-price, must-get-it growth of Reiki in our three-dimensional world, when so much that is "From the highest good—for the highest good" is being abused? The polarity of confusion is clarity. At the 1994 Reiki Association Gathering, Phyllis Lei Furumoto was very aware that we must not allow confusion to blind us to the truth of Reiki. Reiki, when attunement is received, no matter what Master attunes who, and whoever gives it to whom, is always there. It cannot be quantified or rationally structured. Its simplicity defines that it just is, and when given for healing it flows of itself in the right quantity to wherever it is needed. When we can make that shift in consciousness to allow our heart to be in

> alignment with our divinity, when our ego becomes the servant of our soul, then I believe Reiki becomes more. Its potential for healing and for good is vast, far beyond our present limited perception.
>
> Confusion forces us all to look into our own hearts, to question our own integrity. This present confusion has a purpose; as Reiki practitioners and teachers it is a personal and corporate challenge for us to seek clarity, to acknowledge and *be* our own truth—do we *practice* Reiki or *are we* Reiki?

As the facts unfold, the Western Reiki tradition has three choices: to align itself with the Japanese lineage, to cling to our traditional story and lineage, or to find a middle way and allow these two aspects to gradually grow into one movement by acknowledging and valuing our differences and similarities.

Do we need a Grand Master? For those who do, we have a very good one; for those who don't, that is also fine. There is no reason why those who wish to retain and support a Western Reiki Grand Master should not do so. Indeed, many people agree that Phyllis Furumoto is excellent in that role. Perhaps more importantly if we want a Reiki history that is accurate and an insight into Dr. Usui's original intentions, then the translation of the memorial stone story (see following page) is perfect.

The inscription on the memorial stone was written anonymously by one of Dr. Usui's closest disciples. In one section, he says that, "Even now, after Dr. Usui's passing, Reiki will spread far and wide for a long time to come." So he must have realized that one day many people would read his words about Dr. Usui and Reiki. We can therefore assume that he chose his words carefully and that they are heartfelt and accurate.

Toward the end of the inscription the writer says that "I was asked to write these words to help keep his [Dr. Usui's] great work alive." This gives us an indication of the power of the inscription and its relevance to practitioners and especially teachers of Reiki. Regularly reading and contemplating the meaning of the inscription can help us to create a close connection with Dr. Usui and to understand what makes a "successful" Reiki practitioner or teacher.

The following is a translation of the inscription on the Memorial Stone of Dr. Mikao Usui, the Founder of Reiki. Dr. Usui's grave and memorial stone can be found at Saihoji temple in the Toyotama district of Tokyo, Japan.

Dr. Usui's Memorial Inscription

"Someone who studies hard (i.e., practices meditation) and works assiduously to improve body and mind for the sake of becoming a better person is called "a man of great spirit." People who use that great spirit for a social purpose, that is, to teach the right way to many people and do collective good, are called "teachers." Dr. Usui was one such teacher. He taught the Reiki of the universe (universal energy). Countless people came to him and asked him to teach them the great way of Reiki and to heal them.

Dr. Usui was born in the first year of the Keio period, called Keio Gunnen, on August 15th (1864). His first name was Mikao and his other name is pronounced either Gyoho (or Kyoho*). He was born in the village of Yago in the Yamagata district of Gifu prefecture. His ancestor's name is Tsunetane Chiba. His father's name

*Dr. Usui's name may have changed as it was an ancient Japanese custom for a teacher to give a new name to his student in order to break continuity with the past and start anew. Sometimes a new name was adopted by the student himself.

was Uzaemon. His mother's family name was Kawaai From what is known, he was a talented and hard-working student. As an adult he traveled to several Western countries and China to study. He worked arduously, but did at some point run into some bad luck. However he didn't give up and trained himself arduously.

One day he went to Mount Kurama on a twenty-one day retreat to fast and meditate. At the end of this period he suddenly felt the great Reiki energy at the top of his head, which led to the Reiki healing system. He first used Reiki on himself, then tried it on his family. Since it worked well for various ailments, he decided to share this knowledge with the public at large. He opened a clinic in Harajuku, Aoyama-Tokyo, in April of the 11th year of the Taisho period (1921). He not only gave treatment to countless patients, some of whom had come from far and wide, but he also hosted workshops to spread his knowledge. In September of the twelfth year of the Taisho period (1923), the devastating Kanto earthquake shook Tokyo. Thousands were killed, injured, or became sick in its aftermath. Dr. Usui grieved for his people, but he also took Reiki to the devastated city and used its healing powers on the surviving victims. His clinic soon became too small to handle the throng of patients, so in February of the 14th year of the Taisho period (1924), he built a new one outside Tokyo in Nakano.

His fame spread quickly all over Japan, and invitations to distant towns and villages started coming in. Once he went to Kure, another time to Hiroshima prefecture, then to Saga prefecture and Fukuyama. It was during his stay in Fukuyama that he was hit by a fatal stroke on March 9th, of the fifteenth year of the Taisho period (1926). He was 62 years of age.

Dr. Usui had a wife named Sadako, her maiden name was Suzuki. They had a son and a daughter. The son, Fuji Usui took over the family business after Dr. Usui's passing.

Dr. Usui was a very warm, simple and humble person. He was physically healthy and well-proportioned. He never showed off and always had a smile on his face, he was also very courageous in the face of adversity. He was, at the same time, a very cautious person. His talents were many. He liked to read, and his knowledge of medicine, psychology, fortune-telling and theology of religions around the world was vast. This life-long habit of studying and gathering information certainly helped pave the way to perceiving and understanding Reiki. (I think this refers to his experience on Mount Kurama). Reiki not only heals diseases, but also amplifies innate abilities, balances the spirit, makes the body healthy, and thus helps achieve happiness. To teach this to others you should follow the five principles of the Meiji Emperor and contemplate them in your heart.

They should be spoken daily, once in the morning and once in the evening:

1. *Don't get angry today.*
2. *Don't worry today.*
3. *Be grateful today.*
4. *Work hard today (meditative practice).*
5. *Be kind to others today.*

The ultimate goal is to understand the ancient secret method for gaining happiness (Reiki) and thereby discover an all-purpose cure for many ailments. If these principles are followed you will achieve the great tranquil mind of the ancient sages. To begin spreading the Reiki system, it is important to start from a place close to you (yourself), don't start from something distant such as philosophy or logic.

Sit still and in silence every morning and every evening with your hands folded in the "Ghasso" or "Namaste." Follow the great principles, and be clean and quiet. Work on your heart and do things from the quiet space inside of you. Anyone can access Reiki, because it begins within yourself. Philosophical paradigms are changing the world round. If Reiki can be spread throughout the world it will touch the human heart and the morals of society. It will be helpful for many people, and will not only heal disease, but also the Earth as a whole. Over 2,000 people learned Reiki from Dr. Usui More learned it from his senior disciples, and they carried Reiki even further. Even now after Dr. Usui's passing, Reiki will spread far and wide for a long time to come. It is a universal blessing to have received Reiki from Dr. Usui and to be able to pass it on to others. Many of Dr. Usui's students converged to build this memorial here at Saihoji Temple in the Toyotoma district.

I was asked to write these words to help keep his great work alive. I deeply appreciate his work and I would like to say to all of his disciples that I am honored to have been chosen for this task. May many understand what a great service Dr. Usui did to the world."

Dr. Usui's Memorial Inscription is reproduced, with the kind permission of the author and German publisher, from *Reiki Fire* by Frank Arjava Petter. Published by Lotus Light Publications in the USA, and in Germany as *Das Reiki Feuer* by Windpferd Verlagsgesellschaft mbH, Aitrang, Germany.

The above text is by the author and translator, Frank Arjava Petter and his wife Chetna M. Kobayashi. The original translation from traditional to contemporary Japanese was done by Masano Kobayashi, Chetna's mother. Many thanks to them for this special work.

3

First Degree Reiki

There are four levels of Reiki: First Degree, Second Degree, Advanced, and Masters. First Degree teaches us how to use Reiki for ourselves, how to share it with others, and is the primary focus of this book. For many people learning Reiki is a very personal experience. Sometimes Reiki students experience sudden positive changes in their lives whether physically, mentally, emotionally, spiritually, or in other areas such as relationships, careers, and financial matters. For most people, it is the beginning of a gentle but powerful process of improving health, well-being, lifestyle, and self-awareness. Many Reiki practitioners have special memories of their First Degree course, and see it as a major turning point in their lives.

Reiki works in harmony with the individual and the lives of those around them. Reiki can work in dramatic or very subtle and unobtrusive ways so the changes we undergo and the benefits we receive can be immediate or may take time to become apparent. Other people can notice these changes before we do, as it is not always easy to see our own mind, because we are so used to looking "out" rather than within! Certainly if we use Reiki regularly, with a good motivation, we will experience continuing positive changes in ourselves and in all aspects of our lives. Those close to us, too, can receive great benefit, even without actually receiving Reiki treatments.

Healing From Within

Sometimes we may be reluctant to give up old habits that feel "safe" and seem to be part of our identity, so change can appear uncomfortable. If we have not dealt with difficult situations or feelings in the past, Reiki may help us to experience a period of gentle, emotional release, followed by renewed clarity and an ability to put the past in context with our present and future. These changes are really beneficial. The more we open up and trust this process of inner growth, the easier and more enjoyable it will be, and the more skillful we will become at using Reiki to release negative patterns of behavior and adopt more positive habits.

Changing for the better does not have to be painful or take a long time; indeed change is in the nature of all phenomena. Moment by moment, things change; life is a constant cycle of birth, growth, decay, and death. If we can develop the wisdom to realize this, and release our need to control life, our minds will be more relaxed, peaceful, open, and ready to transform difficult situations into opportunities for personal growth. When we actually begin to seek positive change in ourselves—instead of being victims of circumstance—we become part of the solution rather than part of the problem.

Finding a Reiki Master

It's important to find a Reiki Master with whom you feel comfortable. The Reiki Association and the Reiki Alliance can supply details of members who are Reiki Masters, however membership of these organizations does not confer any kind of recommendation and there are many excellent practitioners and Masters who choose not to be part of an association (see Appendix 3 for more information).

Alternatively, many Reiki Masters advertise their courses in health and healing magazines and journals, and on the Internet. Some Reiki Masters also give talks and demonstrations where the public have the opportunity to hear Dr. Usui's story, experience Reiki, and ask questions. Many Reiki Masters give formal treatments on a regular basis. This is another way of trying Reiki and finding a Master that is right for you. It is a good idea to have an informal chat with a few different Masters either face-to-face or by telephone before you decide.

The Reiki Empowerments

First Degree Reiki is usually taught over two days or up to four evenings and is very easy and enjoyable to learn. The size of classes can vary according to the Master's preference and experience; usually between five to fifteen people is normal.

During the training, each person receives four empowerments (or attunements). These open up your subtle mental and physical energy systems and prepare you to channel

Universal Life Force Energy. This process also creates a permanent connection, or gateway, for the Reiki energy to be continually present in our lives. The attunements are gentle, peaceful, and powerful. They take only a few minutes per person. This may not seem long, but the group attunement energy is present in the room during the whole process, so there is plenty of time to receive a very deep, personal healing. The Master will explain how the attunements will be conducted and may gently touch your hands, head, and shoulders while using the four Reiki symbols to activate and complete the attunement process. After the fourth attunement, the recipient is fully empowered and the Reiki energy is established within his or her energy system for life. Reiki will then always be available, and we can choose to use it whenever we wish.

The typical reactions during and after a Reiki attunement are:

- Increased energy
- Inner peace and a feeling of warmth within and/or around the body
- Gentle tingling sensations, especially in the hands, which may also feel hot
- A sense of energy flowing in and around the body
- Clearer senses
- Less stress and emotional problems
- Improved physical health
- Increased ability to deal positively with stressful situations
- A sense of "coming home" and of being in touch with "the flow" of life

- Deepened spiritual awareness and experiences e.g. seeing or sensing auras, energy, colors, etc.
- Increased clarity of mind and deeper intuitive or inner wisdom
- A general feeling of being more whole, healthy, and happy; a more complete sense of "self"

Everyone is different. Some people may feel nothing during an attunement, and this, too, is normal. Reiki works in the way that we need it as individuals. Colors, lights, and amazing experiences are very nice, but not always necessary to gain the most from Reiki. Regular daily practice and long-term personal experience is more valuable. We need deep, long-lasting benefits, instead of short-term highs.

Reiki Flows Naturally

We don't have to think about it, or meditate to make it work. Just by placing our hands on our body, Reiki will naturally flow where we most need it. It really is that simple. As Hawayo Takata once said:

Hands On, Reiki On!
Hands Off, Reiki Off!

If we forget about Reiki, or choose not to use it for some time—even years—Reiki will still work for us simply by:

- Placing our hands on our own body
- Placing our hands on someone or something else
- Making a mental "Reiki" intention; i.e., mentally directing Reiki for a specific purpose other than a hands-on healing. (This is explained in more detail in the next chapter.)

Reiki Responsibility

As we continue to use Reiki, we will naturally discover more effective ways to use and benefit from it, and the greater our healing abilities will become. However, this does not mean that we will become more powerful! It is not possible to use Reiki in a controlling way. Experience shows that negative or manipulative intentions lead to poor relationships, a lower quality of energy, and only short-term results from healing.

We can also be sure that whatever we put out into the world with our actions of body, speech, and mind will come back to us sooner or later. However, Reiki is very forgiving. We can learn much from our mistakes if we have a genuine wish to heal ourselves and others. Reiki can surround us, guide us, and protect us for the rest of our lives and help us to transform our mistakes and difficulties into meaningful lessons, if we wish.

Natural Chakra Balancing

During and after the First Degree attunements, Reiki enters our body and mind through the crown chakra, located on the top of the head, and then through the other major and minor chakras. A chakra is a rotating center of Internal Life Force Energy, a junction where subtle internal energy channels meet and where energy can enter or leave the body or be transformed into a different level of energy. We have seven major chakras running down the center of the body: Crown, Third Eye (forehead), Throat, Heart, Solar Plexus, Sacral (just below navel), and Base chakra (see Figure 3.1).

Each chakra carries a different quality of energy and has specific functions relating to the body and mind. They range in color and quality from Base upward: red, orange, yellow, emerald, blue, violet and gold. Each chakra carries a different quality of energy and has specific functions relating to the body and mind. The presence of Reiki has a very positive effect on the chakras in that it encourages and supports a more open, pure, and efficient creation and transformation of Internal Life Force Energy. As explained earlier, this helps establish a sense of well-being, openness, and clarity of mind. There are many books available on the intricacies

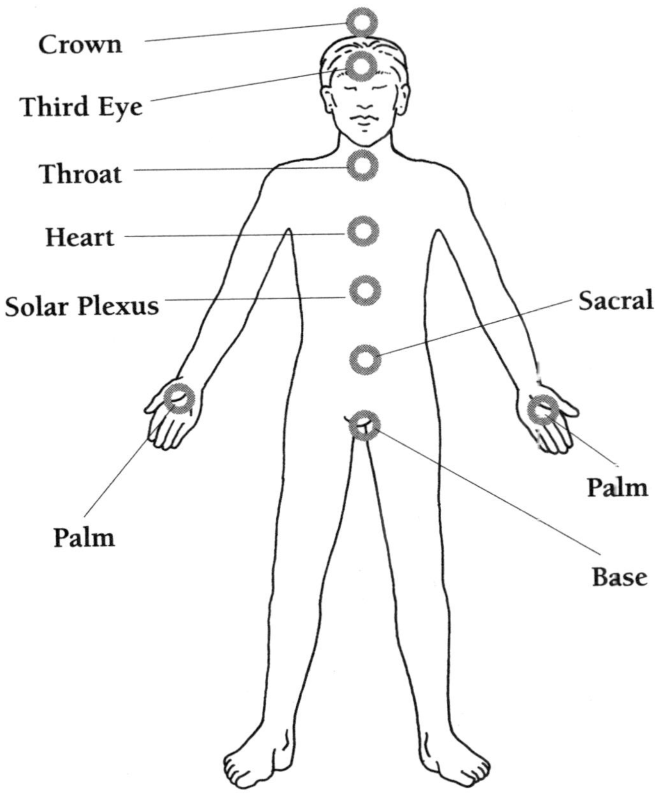

Figure 3.1 Major chakra points on human body and palm chakras

of the human energy system and related healing and meditation techniques. Such knowledge—although often useful—is not necessary for the successful practice of Reiki.

When we give Reiki to ourselves or others, we receive it through our crown chakra and it flows through our energy system, down our arms, and out through our palm chakras. Reiki also seems to "envelop" the practitioner and the person they are treating with a cushion or aura of healing energy that seems to create a special healing environment or atmosphere, while also protecting and encouraging the healing process.

Earth Energy

We also have energy centers, or chakras, on the soles of our feet that allow a life force energy exchange with the Earth. We should be aware that although the Earth does not possess consciousness, like living beings, it is a vital source of External Life Force Energy. The Earth has many energy channels and energy centers running through it in a similar way to the energy system of our own bodies.

There are many special and holy centers of Life Force Energy where the Earth's energies are linked to the Universal Life Force Energy and other realms of existence. These energy sites are often marked by stone circles, religious buildings, statues, old trees, and other monuments. Sometimes they are not obviously marked at all and often they change position and quality with the seasons, and can be affected by other influences, including new buildings or roads.

There is an important reciprocal give-and-receive relationship between the Earth, our own energy system, and the Universal Life Force Energy. We can begin to understand this relationship by studying the life of a tree.

Trees need sunlight and reach up to the source of light with their branches and leaves. Energetically they also draw Universal Life Force Energy from above and External Life Force Energy from the sun. Their roots reach deep into the ground and draw up nutrients, water, and the Earth's External Life Force Energy. Continuous healthy growth is ensured by this balance of energy exchange. It is the perfect middle way towards inner and outer growth, a path that many spiritual practitioners try to emulate in their own lives. The human being is an energy center similar to a tree. We need a balance of Earth Energy and Universal Life Force Energy to enable us to grow in a balanced way on all levels. We can have our head in the clouds as long as we have our feet on the Earth. As we reach toward and receive Reiki, so Reiki begins to open our hearts and minds drawing us toward our own center. We need to keep our feet on the ground to gain the most from our practice and in order to stay in touch with the real world and the needs of others.

If we continue to separate ourselves from this Earth–Heaven relationship by covering more of the Earth in concrete, living in areas where we cannot even see the Earth and not consciously being part of this greater energy exchange, then we can expect poor health and poor states of mind. Giving Reiki to the Earth through our feet is a wonderful way of giving healing to our planet. Not only will your energy benefit all living beings on Earth, through the Earth's own energy system, but you will receive an exchange of "Earth Energy" that will be a very powerful aid to your own healing and personal growth. Again, if we can find a little time to do this regularly the results will be excellent. (See "Meditation for Earth Healing" chapter 9.)

Preparing for First Degree

Reiki can begin to work for us even before we have taken First Degree. Some people go through natural changes in the days leading up to the course; changes involving attitudes, relationships, health, and other issues. Perhaps Reiki can work for us in this way because we have set an intention to move towards Reiki by planning to take First Degree, so creating a mental bridge or connection through which Reiki can touch our lives even before formal training begins.

In fact it is not uncommon to look back over our lives after taking Reiki and see a pattern of events and experiences that almost seem to have lead us to Reiki as the next step in our personal evolution. If we have an interest in the ideas of karma, it is worth considering that our actions of giving healing to others in past lives, and of encouraging others to find a spiritual path may have created the causes for us to find Reiki in this life. (These ideas are discussed in more detail in chapter 8.)

In order to gain the most from a Reiki empowerment, it is helpful to perhaps spend three to seven days preparing yourself mentally and physically for the attunements. This is not essential, so only do it if it feels right for you.

Pre-Attunement Guidelines

Following these guidelines can help to create the right conditions for a smoother transition into Reiki. The thirty-day self-treatment period, after the training course, can also help us gain the most from the powerful healing opportunities that the attunement energy provides.

- Avoid eating any kind of meat prior to and during the attunements

- Don't drink alcohol during this time
- Cut down on smoking, or stop altogether if you are able
- Avoid caffeinated drinks and try to drink lots of uncarbonated mineral water or herbal tea
- Avoid eating chocolate, sweets, or other refined foods
- Eat only fresh food products, and consider a brief water or juice fast, but only if you have experienced fasting
- Reduce time watching television and avoid confrontational or stressful situations
- Keep a peaceful, happy, and relaxed mind
- Spend quiet time on your own in a peaceful place; go for walks in pleasant surroundings
- Meditate or pray for at least twenty minutes each day, or simply spend this time in silence or reading a spiritual text

Essentially approach the attunements with a relaxed and open mind. The attunements will work whether you have followed the above preparations or not, so don't worry if you haven't had enough time; it may just take a little longer for you to receive the full effect of the empowerments.

Occasionally a cleansing of body and mind may occur before, during, or shortly after the First Degree course. This might involve:

- A short, minor illness such as a cold, or influenza
- Sweating
- Headaches

- Frequent urination
- A need to sleep more
- A need to drink more
- Temporary loss or increase in appetite
- Some other minor physical problems
- Some type of emotional release, such as crying or laughing

After the attunements we should give ourselves a full Reiki treatment every day for thirty days. Drinking lots of water or herbal teas and eating healthily during this period can also be helpful. As mentioned a gentle detoxification may occur, but this will usually pass quickly as the body continues to cleanse and rebalance itself. Occasionally this process can take longer, perhaps weeks or months, especially if you have been particularly unhealthy or have had many difficult life experiences.

This is a very positive process and is needed to fully cleanse and heal the system. Occasionally the symptoms of detoxification can appear to get worse the more Reiki we receive, if this happens we should just be patient, remember it is a positive process and it will pass in time. Try doing less Reiki but more often, so instead of a full treatment once a day, try two thirty-minute or three twenty-minute treatments per day and gradually build up to a full treatment in one session. If this is still too much, just do what you feel is right for you and increase the time when you are able to.

"Positive" Fatigue

When some people have completed their First Degree Reiki training, it is quite common for them to feel tired or sleepy for days and occasionally weeks. This is a good sign that you are beginning to learn how to really open and fully relax. Often the amount of stress we carry goes unnoticed as we move from one thing in life to another and layers of stress gradually accumulate in our system, both physically and mentally, to the extent that we never allow ourselves time to just be who we are.

We can even build up and carry stress with us from one lifetime to another for many lifetimes. This accumulated stress acts as a barrier to inner peace or to a sense of our timeless spirituality. Practicing Reiki, meditation, prayer, or deep relaxation is a way to gradually release stress, cleanse the body/mind and re-introduce us to ourselves! This process may happen many times throughout years of Reiki practice as we cleanse and release deeper levels of accumulated stress that may have been laid down long ago.

Learning to open and allowing stress, often in the form of negative thought patterns, to arise and fall away can sometimes be unnerving as we often feel these aspects of our mind are very close to our own center, personal nature, or character. This process can sometimes leave us feeling a little naked and unsure of ourselves. However, given time and a little positive experience we will develop the confidence and wish to consciously seek and appreciate this inner path towards a more whole, healthy, and complete way of living and being.

The path of Reiki, like all paths of personal and spiritual growth, is a lifelong practice. There are no quick fixes and there will be ups and downs. The symptoms of detoxification can return from time to time as we approach more deep-seated mental and emotional obstacles along the way. Being realistic about this can help us be prepared for such obstacles and less disheartened when we appear to be stuck! A great part of the path is learning to transform or see our obstacles as opportunities. This is where Reiki can help us greatly. Rather than avoiding these challenges, we can learn to transform them into the path to inner healing.

How Others React to Reiki

When we first learn Reiki, other people may react differently toward us. Although most people cannot see it, Reiki equates to a high frequency of light that surrounds us in all that we do and the situations we find ourselves in. It also touches the lives of those around us. People may react to this change by either being much more friendly, or even *unfriendly* toward us. On some subconscious level others are aware that we are carrying this "light" and on the whole will want to benefit from it.

If anyone is unusually critical or unfriendly, just accept it without judgment—again it will pass. Also if others are unusually demanding of your time, try to strike a balance by allowing people to draw Reiki through you but not to the extent that your time becomes conditional, i.e., "you expect something in return." If you think this might happen, it is better to give someone a "formal" Reiki treatment in return for an appropriate amount of money or another type of fair exchange. A fair exchange is one that leaves both parties feeling good about giving.

If you are "challenged" about Reiki, by your partner, friends, family, or others, then remain calm and centered when explaining yourself. Be honest about why you are doing Reiki. If you are speaking from a place of truth—your truth—then others will more readily accept and support what you are doing, even if at first it seems a little unorthodox. Staying centered and speaking your truth is easier if you value yourself and what you are doing and treat others in the same way. If you feel threatened by others' doubt or derision, this can be a good opportunity to deepen your understanding and connection with Reiki. Ask yourself questions like: Why have I chosen to do Reiki? What does Reiki mean to me?

If you feel clear and sure of your position, then you can be open and honest without fear of judgment or rejection.

Sharing a Reiki Exchange

Within a few weeks of taking First Degree Reiki, there may be an opportunity to meet with your teacher, your First Degree group, and other Reiki practitioners at a "Reiki Exchange." This is a very special gathering. It will give you the opportunity to ask any questions and share your experiences with others. When many Reiki people come together, the level of energy is more than multiplied by the number present. It is a great opportunity to give and receive a high quality of healing energy.

The first part of the evening is usually for simple meditation and sending Reiki as a group to world situations, friends, and family. The rest of the time is spent treating each other in groups of about four, so three people will work on one person for approximately fifteen minutes each. This can be a very powerful experience, so before you receive Reiki think briefly how you would like the energy to work for you. What areas of your life need Reiki? Then set a clear and appropriate mental intention to direct the energy to these situations for the greatest good. If your Reiki Master does not run an Exchange, the Reiki Association or Reiki Alliance may be able to help you (see Appendix 3 for more information).

You should feel able to contact your Reiki Master at any time if you have any questions without necessarily waiting for the next Exchange. Although Reiki is a very simple technique to learn, it's unlikely that you will have all your questions answered during the course, so spend some time to review what you have covered, make notes of any questions that arise for you and use them to take your next step.

First Degree Reiki is often the first introduction that many people have to New Age ideas, and the processes and techniques of personal growth. It's also a good way to meet other people who are interested in these fields. It is important not to take on too much at once. Be practical. Keep your feet on the ground, and your Reiki practice simple and clear. If all the "New Age stuff" is a bit too much, then just be very selective and take your time to sort out the gold from the dross.

Further Reiki Training

Further training is not essential to gain the most from Reiki. Many people are very happy with the benefits they receive from First Degree Reiki and do not wish to move on any further. If used wisely, First Degree Reiki will bring you all that you need in terms of healing capabilities and spiritual progression for the rest of your life.

However, if you would like to enhance the power of Reiki available to you and become more consciously involved in the process of your own evolution, then it is worth considering further training.

Second Degree Reiki Training

Second Degree Reiki is usually taught over two half-days, or two evenings. There are two attunements, which are similar to the First Degree ones, and three symbols to learn. You are taught how to create and activate the symbols and how to use them to enhance your healing abilities and your general use of Reiki. The symbols enable you to direct Reiki for specific purposes, enhance mental and emotional healing, and send absentee Reiki to anyone, anywhere in the world. You can even send Reiki to past or future events!

Although it differs with each student, the Second Degree energy is generally about four times stronger than First Degree. Usually a period of at least two-to-three months is required between First and Second Degree training, as this allows the practitioner time to adjust physically and mentally to First Degree and prepares them to make the most of the new attunements and increased level of energy with Second Degree.

Learning Advanced Reiki

This is a big step to take! Usually practitioners wait at least six months after taking Second Degree before considering Advanced. However, if you feel it is the right time for you, and the opportunity arises, don't hesitate! With this level of energy we can achieve and experience amazing results in our own process of self-discovery and in the ways we perceive and understand people and the world around us.

The quality of the energy we carry with Advanced Reiki is much finer or higher, more powerful, and yet more subtle. There are two more attunements and the Reiki Master Symbol is also given to the student, its meaning and uses are fully explained.

Becoming a Reiki Master

This level of Reiki is intended for those who specifically wish to teach Reiki to others, whether only a few students per year or regular classes. If you already have the Master Symbol from Advanced Reiki you will be taught how to attune others and teach the different levels of Reiki.

Being a Reiki Master is a special vocation, although you don't have to be a very special person to be a Master! Often the best Reiki teachers are simply those who genuinely want to help others and wish to commit themselves to the processes and challenges of a life close to the heart of Reiki.

4

Using Reiki

Once you have taken First Degree Reiki you can choose how and when to use the energy. Here are four basic guidelines that may help you:

1. Intention—Reiki energy naturally follows thought.
2. Reiki is infinite.
3. Reiki always works for the greatest good.
4. Dedication—The future effects of Reiki actions.

1. Intention—Reiki Energy Naturally Follows Thought

As explained earlier, our thoughts and feelings ride on internal energies, similar to frequencies of light or a very subtle inner wind. Indeed, sometimes when we receive Reiki we can feel its subtle presence in and around the body almost like a very gentle air current, often moving in a circular or spiral motion.

Without physical energy produced from good food, clean water, or physical exercise, we would not enjoy good health. Likewise without the right conditions and care of our internal energies, we cannot enjoy good mental and emotional health. If we don't use our mind in a positive and creative way, and surround ourselves with negative influences like violent films or damaging relationships, we can expect our internal energies and our mind to degenerate, like a muscle that is unused.

Our ability to direct our thoughts and actions depends upon the mental faculty of intention. If we wish to do something mentally or physically, we begin with an idea or feeling, which needs internal energy to arise from the subtle or subconscious mind to our surface consciousness. Only then can our internal energies carry and support subsequent thoughts and feelings as they arise, and we develop our ideas leading to a decision for a course of mental, verbal, or physical action. This conscious decision is our intention. We are usually unaware of this process as it happens spontaneously throughout the day. We may, for example, feel thirsty, have an idea to make a cup of tea, and then decide to go and make one!

The process may become more obvious when we think deeply about a subject, meditate, receive or give Reiki, or work out a solution to a particular problem. We can compare this natural process to driving a car. The internal energies are like the car we drive, and we are able to direct the car by making judgments, decisions, and actions in order to get to our intended destination.

Simply taking a walk in the fresh air can help to clear our thoughts—the influence of fresh Life Force Energy and gentle exercise on our own internal energies and processes of thought are very positive. Even if we live in urban area, regular exercise such as walking, swimming, Yoga, or Tai Chi can greatly improve our capacity to create and channel pure energy.

Greatest Results with Least Resources

Whatever activity we take on, generally we want to achieve the greatest results while using the least resources. Our success in this depends on the quality and strength of our intention and the quality and power of our internal energy. Reiki's main purpose is to improve the power and quality of our internal energy by "plugging us into" the Universal Life Force Energy. On a deep subconscious level, this energy is part of our own inner nature. It pervades the whole of space and time; it is always spontaneously new, perfect, and yet ancient, timeless, and unchanging. It seeks to help and support us in becoming all that we truly are, if that is what we wish! The main intention of this boundless compassion and wisdom is the expansion of happiness, fulfillment, and knowledge for all living beings.

Once we are empowered with Reiki, our thoughts, feelings, and actions become powerful and more effective in realizing our intentions. Reiki will naturally bring us what we wish for without us necessarily having to strive or work so hard for it, provided our wishes are wise and truly beneficial for ourselves and others.

It is the responsibility of individual Reiki practitioners to use this energy wisely, and to make the most of "carrying" Reiki. We can use Reiki to take responsibility for our own health and to improve our thoughts, feelings, and actions. Although we cannot easily see it, whatever we think and feel about ourselves and others has a direct effect upon everything in creation. Because energy follows thought, sooner or later, the effects of our thoughts and actions will become our reality.

When our thoughts and feelings are energized with Reiki, we can quickly achieve positive changes in our lives. All we need is a consistent, stable, and honest wish or sincere intention to improve our quality of life. Reiki will do the rest!

Generally we can use specific, clear wishes or intentions for how we would like to use Reiki, or we can simply and regularly think:

I would like to use Reiki in everything I do, to improve my quality of life and help my family, friends, and everyone I meet.

In this way, all our actions of body, speech, and mind will be blessed and surrounded by Reiki. Like Dr. Usui, we will gradually become a real "lighthouse," a source of positive energy in a world that greatly needs light.

The Power of Communal Reiki

When two or more Reiki people come together to discuss their progress, the level of energy present is more than doubled, similar to the effect of a Reiki Exchange. Conversation can be inspired and touched with great wisdom and insight. Perhaps the power of a group sharing a common intent to increase wisdom and understanding is greater than that generated by an individual.

When such a meeting occurs either spontaneously or on a regular basis, all the participants come away feeling energized and uplifted. Often obstacles or issues they have been trying to deal with alone are removed, or they are more clear on a proper solution. This process of creative, community-generated insight and healing has a good effect on the surrounding neighborhood. Positive energy is sent out in waves from the group to the whole area and beyond. This can indirectly help reduce community stress and even crime, thereby creating the right conditions for a more harmonious living environment.

2. *Reiki is Infinite*

Reiki can never be depleted. The more we use it in the right way, the greater our capacity to channel pure light. The more we become aware of the possibilities that Reiki makes available to us, the more we can achieve them. Reiki can take us as far as we want to go in whatever we wish to do. Reiki will never put us in a situation that we are unable to transform into a learning and life-enhancing experience. All we need is a little courage, positive motivation, and a happy mind!

We don't have to limit our intentions; we can have as many as we wish, or just one. We can set intentions for minor things like finding a parking space, or for more important things like personal growth and relationship issues. On a greater scale we can use Reiki for healing conflicts or disasters locally, nationally, and globally. The more we use Reiki, the more powerful and effective our actions will be, and the wiser and more skillful our intentions will become.

We can direct the energy consciously simply by creating a clear mental intention. We don't have to visualize, meditate, or develop deep concentration. We just need a clear idea of what we want to achieve. Sometimes we do need time to think and create the right intention, and it may help then to give ourselves hands-on Reiki for a few minutes while thinking:

How can I use Reiki in this situation?
What would be an appropriate and clear Reiki intention for this situation?

This is a powerful way to actually set specific intentions or send Reiki to a particular situation, problem, person, or issue. Simply place your hands on your body for a short time, bring the person or situation to mind and as you feel Reiki coming into your own body and mind imagine and feel that Reiki surrounds and penetrates the thoughts and issues you are concerned with, you don't need to create clear mental images, so don't concentrate too hard, just relax, open your heart and mind. Allow Reiki to work naturally and trust that whatever happens will be for the greatest good, and it will!

Ideas for Using Reiki

Here are a few examples of how we can use Reiki either as a hands-on healing technique, or by setting intentions:

- Healing ourselves and others physically, mentally, and emotionally
- Spiritual and personal growth, developing compassion, wisdom, patience, and empathy
- Healing animals and plants
- Relationship problems at work or home
- Send Reiki to world situations such as political conflicts, natural disasters, traffic accidents, or local situations like crime, unemployment, or poverty

- Combine Reiki with other complementary therapies such as Aromatherapy or Reflexology
- Finding new employment or career, a new house, car, or anything else we may need
- To have good weather on holiday or any other time
- To have a safe and swift journey when driving or traveling generally, or to find a parking space
- To find a solution to any specific problem
- Treat yourself before going into stressful situations such as exams, interviews, public speaking, etc.
- Give Reiki to your food before you eat it clothes before you wear them, vitamins and healing to improve their health-giving properties; also use Reiki to energize and cleanse healing crystals
- To be more creative, to improve your memory or learning capacity or any other mental or emotional quality
- To find new ways to use Reiki or to attract people who need Reiki
- To have a peaceful and fulfilling life
- To always be blessed, guided, and protected
- To deepen your experience of Reiki and your own level of self awareness
- For your family, friends, and others to be happy and content

Do We Need Faith?

We can use Reiki as we wish; the only limits are from our own side, those that we create either consciously or subconsciously. We do not need faith for it to work. Children, plants, and animals benefit from Reiki as much as adults. They do not have limiting belief systems, and are not aware of what Reiki might or might not be.

However, if we strongly believe that Reiki will not work for us, perhaps because on some level we don't want our situation to improve or because we still need that situation to develop some inner qualities, then this can create a mental barrier between us and the benefits that Reiki can provide. An open mind and a willingness to learn, adapt, and transform ourselves, rather than the external world, will greatly help our Reiki practice.

3. Reiki Always Works for the Greatest Good

Reiki can never be used for a negative purpose because it only works for the greatest good. Positive energy can only be used for a positive purpose. If our Reiki intentions are motivated by negative selfishness, they will simply not be fulfilled.

Conversely, if our Reiki intentions are truly motivated by positive selflessness our wishes will easily be fulfilled. It is important that we recognize our future is shaped by our present and past actions. Using Reiki with a good motivation will ensure a positive outcome in the future and will help us stop repeating past negative habits.

Breaking the Chain

Since mind or consciousness is often a creature of habit, we can retrain ourselves to become naturally positive by keeping good intentions and not allowing our thoughts, feelings, words, and actions to be motivated by selfish, negative habits. "Breaking the chain," however, does not mean we should suppress negative thoughts and emotions. If they exist within us, they need to be regularly addressed and resolved in a clear, open, and creative way, without over-indulging them or directing them at another person.

If you are overwhelmed by your issues, remember whatever you are experiencing—good or bad—it will pass. Try not to overcomplicate things. Simply by looking for a peaceful mind and developing concern for other people's problems makes our own difficulties less real. Love, compassion, patience, giving, and wisdom can become our normal states of mind no matter how negative we feel or how difficult our life has been. It can take time to change our mental habits, but if our wish is strong and continuous, we can use Reiki to achieve great results often more swiftly than we would expect.

For the Greatest Good

It is generally easier for Reiki to help us if our wishes will benefit others as well as ourselves. Reiki will work most effectively if we can identify the intentions that are for our greatest good and for the greatest good of all. If Reiki is not working for us, we need to be honest in checking our motivation. Is it truly beneficial for ourselves and others, or is there a subtle element of selfishness present? The best way to learn this is simply through practice, experience, and by discussing our insights and problems with others in an open and supportive environment. Reiki gives us the power to achieve great things, but we need to develop the wisdom to know what great things are and how to achieve them in a way that is beneficial for everyone.

Since the main purpose of Reiki is "the greatest good," if we are unsure what intention to set for a particular situation, we can simply think:

May Reiki work for the greatest good
in this situation.

The best specific Reiki intents are simple, clear, and straight from the heart. Since Reiki is an expression of perfect love, it allows us complete freedom to make as many mistakes as we need and this gives us the space to learn through experience. The more we use Reiki with a good motivation, the greater will be our ability to manifest our intentions swiftly and easily.

For our specific intentions to be for the greatest good we need to develop wisdom. Wisdom is not intelligence. Since all living beings wish to avoid suffering and experience only happiness, wisdom is simply the ability to understand which mental, verbal, and physical actions will bring lasting happiness. To achieve this we should understand that happiness is simply a state of mind. Although it appears that happiness comes from the right job, house, relationship, or environment, if we think carefully we will realize that happiness, contentment, and fulfillment come from within and are not dependent upon external objects, particular situations, or other people. If we can use Reiki to help us steadily develop these states of mind instead of trying to manipulate the world around us, our wisdom will increase, our lives will be more peaceful, and we will naturally benefit others in all that we do.

Happiness from Within

Developing happiness from within does not mean we should abandon the external world, but simply see it for what it is: impermanent, transitory, and forever changing. We can combat the turbulence of life by simply generating peaceful minds of compassion, love, patience, giving, joy, and understanding. If we can make these states of mind our best friends, they will never desert us, we will always be prepared for life's challenges and still be able to appreciate good fortune and all that this life has to offer us without depending on it for our happiness.

If we have a particular problem and are wondering how to use Reiki for the greatest good and if we are serious about looking for happiness from within, then to help us gain clarity it can be helpful to ask ourselves three questions:

Do I want things to change ? (reactive)
Do I want to change things ? (proactive)
Do I want to change ? (in- or "inner"-active!)

It is usually better to change ourselves rather than change a situation or expect someone else to change. To find happiness, most people try to change many different things in their lives: their appearance, their job, their partner, the amount of wealth they possess, etc. But these external changes only bring temporary happiness, before long we are looking for something else to relieve the discontentment. In the long run, perhaps over many lifetimes, these unskillful actions actually cause more unhappiness.

Happiness depends upon the mind. However we change our physical world, we will never be satisfied; there will always be something else we will want, or want to change. Most of us play the "I'll-be-happy-when . . ." game: "I'll be happy when I've found the right partner," "I'll be happy when I've found the right job," "I'll be happy when my health improves," etc.

We can be happy right now—whatever our circumstances—simply by *being* happy!

Training in Happiness

Each of us has exactly what we need to be happy. We have exactly the right problems and difficult circumstances we need in order to train in happiness. For example, if we live or work with someone we find irritating, then we could use this as an opportunity to change ourselves and develop the inner qualities of patience, understanding, and perhaps eventually friendship. Looking for a new job or wishing that the other person would leave is not an answer, only a means to escape from or ignore our own shortcomings that we take with us wherever we go, even in to our next life!

Our external difficulties are a reflection of our internal weaknesses. If we are easily irritated by minor problems, then we need to develop tolerance and patience. If we never seem to get what we want, we need to develop contentment with what we have. If we find life threatening, we need to develop confidence, inner strength, and develop the wish to protect others, although not necessarily physically. The more we try to control and manipulate our environment in order to compensate for, or ignore, our weaknesses, the more we attract the things that we wish to avoid.

Most of us are taught at an early age how to avoid our inner world and look for happiness from the external world. Society is like a fairground, full of superficially attractive distractions and diversions that prevent us finding the time, peace, or space to develop a real relationship with ourselves. Our whole lives can easily be filled with the events of birth, childhood, education, career, relationships, family, retirement, old age, and death without ever having a chance to get to *know* who we are. Often it takes illness or other serious, even life-threatening events, to make us sit up and take notice of what is really important and valuable.

Many people spend their whole lives running away from themselves, continually distracted and habitually transferring their attention from one thing in life to the next trying to find happiness in one place and then another. This is only half living, and because many people are doing it, that doesn't make it right. We should be mature enough to look around us, investigate and ask questions about the nature of our own reality and how we can improve our experience of it in a lasting way. We need to have the insight and courage to learn from our own experience and from the wisdom of those who have traveled the same road before us, and we need the understanding and compassion to recognize the suffering of others and act to alleviate it whenever possible.

Getting Out of the Human "Race"

If we stop the game and get off the merry-go-round we can look back at the "human race" chasing its tail and see it for what it really is: a waste of a very special opportunity. A human life is an incredibly rare, fragile, and precious gift. By using our time to train in and deepen our wisdom and happiness, life provides us with an opportunity to transform the endless rounds of major and minor problems.

Many of our problems can be solved by simply getting to know our own mind. The problems that we cannot easily solve can be used to our advantage. By learning to uplift and change ourselves in difficult situations, we can really begin to capitalize on these opportunities and use them to strengthen our good qualities and develop inner happiness. By doing this we can transform everyday situations into the path to lasting happiness. Also, by changing our mind, external situations often change automatically! We need to grasp this opportunity to change direction, turn ourselves around, and look at the world in a different way, we need to think:

Happiness is not *Out There,* it's *In Here.*

Reiki is a key that can help us unlock the door to continuous inner happiness, the treasure that we are all seeking but looking for in the wrong place!

Walking the Middle Way

If you want to use Reiki to walk the path of personal transformation, remember it is a *middle way.* We know that changing habits that have been built up over many years can take time, so be gentle with yourself. Don't expect too much too soon. Keep a happy, peaceful, relaxed mind and a positive motivation, and everything will be possible. If we use Reiki in this way, everything we need will come to us and our path to complete happiness will be swift, smooth, and successful.

4. Dedication— The Future Effects of Reiki Actions

Everything we do, say, and think, every action of body, speech, and mind, creates a potential in the mind for a corresponding physical, verbal, or mental reaction in the future. It also creates the habit or tendency for us to repeat such actions in the future and an increased wish or compulsion to keep performing similar negative actions. If we perform negative actions, we can expect negative reactions sooner or later. Also, if we generally have a negative approach to life we are more likely to create the conditions that attract problems and more difficult circumstances.

Likewise the positive energy we create, by developing patience, kindness, and giving Reiki, for example, will return to us as a very positive experience in one form or another. If we consciously dedicate or direct this positive energy for a specific purpose, this can be a very powerful way of manifesting our intentions, achieving our goals, and accelerating our spiritual and personal growth. Whenever we create positive energy by helping others in any way or by consciously developing positive states of mind, we can dedicate this energy.

Choosing a direction for dedication is similar to creating a Reiki intent. If you choose a purpose that will benefit many people then this wish will be fulfilled more easily than a purely selfish purpose. To dedicate after any positive action, simply think:

May this positive energy be fully dedicated for the greatest good of all

or,

May every living being benefit from this positive energy

Perhaps the greatest goals we could wish for are:

Through the force of this positive energy may every living being be released from suffering and may we all find true lasting happiness swiftly and easily

or,

Through the force of these positive actions may my wisdom and compassion continually increase.

Dedicating the positive energy created by our actions only takes a short time, but this small gesture is a very special practice. We can easily waste or destroy the potential of previous positive actions simply by developing negative states of mind like anger, guilt, or jealousy.

Sincere dedication is like "banking" or protecting the potential of our positive actions for our own and others' future benefit. In this way the potential of our good thoughts, words, and deeds can only increase and will produce excellent results for everyone in the future.

5

Self-Treatment

We can only be effective healers if we can heal ourselves. As part of this process it is important to give ourselves a full Reiki treatment every day for the first thirty days following the First Degree training. By doing this, we adjust mentally and physically to the new energy we carry and it helps us become a clearer channel for Reiki.

You will recall Dr. Usui's first two treatments were upon himself: when he stubbed his toe running down the mountain, and when he was able to eat a large meal after a long fast without becoming ill. These self-healings are very symbolic and should teach us not to be in a rush to "heal the world" but to nourish and develop ourselves well if we are to help others effectively.

The Way of Reiki

Some people will feel able to give Reiki treatments to others immediately after their First Degree attunements. Reiki comes from a limitless source and does not deplete, but generally increases our own energy levels. The process of becoming a pure Reiki channel is continuous and can involve periods of inner cleansing that require rest and self-treatment. Each Reiki practitioner has to assess his or her own requirements and with experience you will be able to judge when it is appropriate to receive rather than give. Receiving can be an act of giving if our motivation is to benefit others. If our real motivation is good, and we have to be very clear and honest with ourselves about this, then our actions will naturally benefit others, even if they sometimes appear to be selfish.

When we give Reiki to others we also receive as much as we need. If we feel ready to treat others on a regular basis, after an appropriate time of self-treatment, then this can really accelerate, enhance, and deepen our *own* growth and development. The longer we continue this practice, along with self-treatment and receiving Reiki from others, the greater our understanding and experience of the way of Reiki will become. This process can also be enriched and supported through regular Reiki Exchanges with other practitioners, perhaps once a month, or more frequently according to your needs.

Intention and Dedication

The quality of our intention directly affects the results of our actions. If we give ourselves Reiki with the wish that everyone benefit from it, then this will create much greater positive energy than if we only wish for our own benefit. If this greater energy is also sincerely dedicated, then sooner or later it will come back to us as a very positive experience and achieve excellent results for everyone. To make the most of a self-treatment, we should set a positive intent before we begin and dedicate when we have finished.

To set our intent, we simply think—at the start of the treatment—of those areas of our lives that we wish to heal, change, or gain clarity on, or again we can set clear specific intents. Our intents can be as great and all-encompassing as we wish. We can also bring to mind specific people we may wish to help, for example we could think:

> *May this treatment benefit, my children, my parents, my partner, the rest of my family, friends, and neighbors (you can mention them by name), everyone in this town, city, and country, everyone on this continent, planet, and all living beings for their greatest good.*

There is no need to constantly reaffirm our intent once we have set it, as this will not increase the power of Reiki and may prevent us relaxing fully and receiving what we need. However, sometimes it may feel right to meditate more deeply on our intentions throughout the treatment. Again knowing when to do this will come with experience. When you wish to do this it may help to sit up in a meditation posture while treating yourself (see chapter 9 for basic meditation techniques). When the treatment is over, we dedicate by thinking of a specific goal or general purpose to which we mentally direct the positive energy we have created through using Reiki. Again the best intentions and dedications are simple, honest, and straight from the heart.

Remember:

Intention

Reiki Action/Treatment

Dedication

Breaking Negative Thought Patterns

By treating ourselves regularly, our health and positive qualities naturally improve. We become more peaceful and less likely to react negatively to difficult situations. This peace also brings an inner confidence and strength, and an increased awareness of our natural talents and abilities. We also become more mentally and emotionally aware and able to recognize our negative thought patterns, and our power to transform them improves, enabling us to become less of a slave to our bad habits!

In short, our mental health improves and, as we find the courage to change ourselves and our lives, we begin to feel good about who we are, where we are, and what we are doing. Regular self-treatment can also act as a preventative health measure. It is well known that reduced stress levels and a sense of well-being can have a positive effect on our physical and mental health.

The Twelve Basic Positions

A full self-treatment lasts sixty minutes. There are twelve basic positions: we place our hands for five minutes in each position (see figures on pages 90–99). The basic positions correspond to the seven major chakras, or energy centers, of the human body. Although the energy will go to those areas of body and mind most in need, each hand position has a more specific effect. If you or someone you are treating has issues they would like to address directly, it is useful to know which positions to spend more time treating (see chapter 8, pages 163–167, for more details).

If you stay in one position for longer than five minutes, you should still spend a full five minutes in each of the other positions, if you have time. Also, don't be afraid to experiment with new positions that feel right and produce good results. After you have practiced Reiki for some time, try reversing the order of the twelve basic positions so that you are working up the body instead of down, as this can help release energy blocks. Also try using only those positions that you feel need Reiki, for this can help us to develop intuitive wisdom and energy awareness. Increasing these abilities also gradually leads to a more subtle awareness and understanding of the mind, the key to all our problems and potential.

The Right Place and Time

Before beginning a self-treatment, create the right environment. Give yourself a suitable period of uninterrupted time, perhaps early morning or evening, preferably at the same time every day. Some people are physically and mentally energized by Reiki and others are left feeling relaxed and ready to unwind, so it is important to choose a time that fits your daily schedule. This reaction can be controlled to some extent by setting the appropriate intent, but it is better to work with the energy and your natural inclinations, rather than against them.

Find a quiet room. Try to avoid potential distractions, by unplugging the telephone or letting an answering machine take your calls, and asking others not to disturb you during your treatment. This is your own time and it is important to value yourself enough not to allow distractions. Have a blanket ready if you think you might get cold. Have relaxing music playing if you enjoy it. You could place a pillow under your knees, as well as your head. This can help take the pressure off a back problem. A clock that is easy to see and that counts five-minute intervals is useful, as it is easy to lose track of time, or fall asleep. If you fall asleep before you have finished, this generally means you needed more Reiki in whatever position you fell asleep. Just carry on from where you left off and complete the treatment, if you have time.

During the Treatment

Keep your fingers and thumbs together, but not tightly. This concentrates the healing in one area and allows a smooth flow of energy. This way of gently stretching the fingers, especially the second or longest finger, stimulates the palm chakras. We can also stimulate the palm chakras by gently massaging the palms in a circular motion or by drawing a counterclockwise spiral in the air above them. Our palm chakras are quite sensitive to energy, so if you point the fingers of one hand at the palm of the other without touching it and move them in a circular or spiral motion, you may feel a tingling sensation or movement in the palm. Once you have taken the Reiki empowerments, you become more sensitive to energy and your own life-force energy level increases.

When giving yourself Reiki try to make each position as comfortable as possible by using pillows, cushions, and a blanket if necessary. Try not to break contact with your body while changing hand positions, as this restricts the free flow of energy and interrupts the process of deep relaxation. We can treat ourselves either lying down or sitting up—whichever enables you to cover all the positions comfortably while staying relaxed. If you have weak arm muscles or a shoulder or neck injury, it is possible to do the first two positions lying on your side with a pillow between your elbows to support the arms. Roll over and change sides between the first and second position to allow the energy to balance and flow freely through your body and aura. Some of the back positions may be difficult to reach so you can either put your hands as close to the correct position as possible, or spend longer on the corresponding front position. Alternatively, do the front positions again and set a clear mental intention for the energy to go through to the back. Again this may be especially helpful for people with neck, shoulder, and back problems.

Self-treatment can be combined with other self-help techniques such as affirmations, visualizations, Aromatherapy, or Bach Flower Remedies. Experiment and enjoy finding the most effective combinations for you. Combining Reiki with crystals can be especially powerful, but be careful! Make sure you use the right crystals, in the right places, for the right purposes, by reading an appropriate book. However, don't let this stifle your intuition. If you feel it is right to use a crystal in a particular way, try it. Remember that Reiki is a complete system of healing for body and mind; always trying something different can be a diversion from facing and dealing with our real issues. If you use Reiki regularly with an honest wish to "move on" you will receive all that you need and more in terms of healing and personal growth. However, if you are looking for something more, perhaps the best compliment to Reiki is the practice of a recognized path of meditation or prayer. Meditation can enhance and deepen our use of Reiki as well as bringing us other special benefits!

Care After the Treatment and Continuing Self-Treatment

When your self-treatment is over and you have dedicated, get up slowly and take time to "ground" yourself. This allows your energies to balance and your mind to become clear before returning to daily activity. Rushing around directly after deep relaxation can leave you feeling vulnerable, light-headed, and even irritable. Everyone is different and it may take some people longer to come round after a treatment. If you feel particularly sensitive, vulnerable, or light-headed after a treatment, then just sit up for a while and set an intent like:

Balanced, centered, grounded, and fully protected.

This is also a good intent to use at any other time, especially if your are going into a situation where you might be challenged by others. Also giving Reiki to your feet or forehead may reduce dizziness. It is also good practice to wash your hands after a treatment, and a shower feels great if you have the time.

After the first thirty days, we do not need to do a full treatment every day, although many people continue this practice as they notice a difference if they reduce the time they spend with Reiki. If on some days you don't have much time, then even a little Reiki is better than none. If you can make some regular time available every day for Reiki, perhaps twenty to thirty minutes if you are busy, give yourself a full treatment once or twice a week, then the positive effects will be continuous and long lasting. If you only have a short time available for a general overall treatment just choose three positions; perhaps the back of your head, your heart, and hips, and do five minutes in each position. Set an intention to receive whatever you need, however you need it, during that time, always for your greatest good. Using this type of simple intention we can achieve surprisingly good results in only a short time.

Sometimes we may feel that we want to give ourselves a lot of Reiki perhaps many hours per day. This is fine for short periods of time, such as a few days or occasionally a few weeks. This can be especially useful in helping us deal with traumatic events like the end of a close relationship, bereavement, serious illness, etc. However, continuing this type of treatment for long periods can sometimes be a subconscious way of diluting the effectiveness of Reiki and using it as a crutch or as a way to avoid life, rather than as a powerful tool for inner healing and personal growth towards responsibility and maturity. This is one of the reasons why the one-hour twelve position treatment is so valuable. For First Degree practitioners, and many advanced practitioners, it is the most effective, efficient, and powerfully transforming way to use Reiki.

Reiki Anytime, Anyplace

You can give yourself Reiki almost anywhere if you have a spare five or ten minutes. This is especially useful in stressful situations like traffic jams, before an interview, after an argument, and before or after any difficult situation. It is probably wiser, if you have the opportunity, to give yourself Reiki before stressful situations arise and set an intent for the situation and all the people involved to receive Reiki for the greatest good. This really will make a difference and ensures a more peaceful, balanced, and fair outcome for all concerned. Remember, all you have to do is place your hands anywhere on your own body and think briefly and clearly how you would like to use Reiki. If you are in a public place and feel people might be wondering what you are doing, then just place your hands on your legs as this is the least obvious position, if you are sitting down.

Use Reiki, bring it through as much as you can and learn to integrate it with your daily life, don't restrict your practice to formal treatments. Finding time for Reiki is not a problem, it just needs a little thought, for example, give yourself Reiki:

- while watching television
- while sitting in a park, or in church
- during tea or lunch break at work
- when traveling by bus, train, or in a car sitting in a traffic jam
- while reading, studying, or memorizing
- when walking anywhere, standing in a line

Learn to consciously empower your life with Reiki. You can call on Reiki anytime; it's there to help you achieve your full potential simply and easily. The more you can relax, open up, and trust Reiki, the more effectively it can work for you. Don't restrict your practice to formal self-treatment. Wherever you are, whatever you are doing and whenever you need it, just set your intent, and Reiki will be with you.

Whenever you have a minor physical problem just place your hands on that part of your body for a few minutes. For example, place your hands on your head for a headache or on your stomach for a stomachache! If you feel stressed, nervous, or confused, try to find where this feeling is centered in your body, such as your stomach, heart, or head, then place your hands there for a few minutes to relieve the problem. Never do Reiki in the bath or swimming pool; you may fall asleep. If you intend to drive after a treatment, make sure you are fully alert.

Reiki's Effect on the Mind

The benefits of regular self-treatment flow over into all areas of our lives. We can bring the deep peace we feel during self-treatment into the rest of our day-to-day life. This is definitely possible and will come with regular practice. Since our tendencies toward positive or negative actions gradually change with our habits of thinking and feeling, if we are able each day to familiarize ourselves with deep peace and happiness, no matter how negative we have been in the past, we cannot avoid becoming more contented and fulfilled. The more we are able to live this way the easier it will be over time to release and heal the burdens of past physical, mental or emotional trauma, and illness. Each day we can become more "present," whole, and complete human beings.

Reiki quiets and settles the mind, allowing us quite naturally to transcend our surface or superficial awareness and touch our innermost being. We only normally reach this level of consciousness during deep sleep. Most people do not recall this because we are not conscious while experiencing it. The sense of deep peace and clarity we sometimes consciously experience during self-treatment arises because we experience deeper levels of mind. This is due to the close dependent relationship between our internal energies and our mind as explained in the first chapter.

As our internal energies become purer and more subtle through self-treatment, so does our mind. As the quality of these internal energies is raised or refined by regular Reiki, this in turn gives rise to the experience of transcending or moving toward our inner nature. It has a positive effect on our physical health because the subsequent reduced levels of physical and mental stress immediately cause our own healing and regenerative abilities to regain their natural power.

Footprints in the Sand

From Buddhism, we know that any illness, before manifesting on the physical or conscious level, initially arises from the very subtle or deepest levels of mind—the subconscious to most people. Ultimately we can only remove the true causes of illness by knowing, experiencing, and purifying our very subtle mind of all the potential seeds of illness created by our own past negative actions of body or mind in previous lives.

Reiki can help remove these seeds; however, the mental imprints of these past actions still remain in the mind—like footprints in the sand—and these create the mental tendencies to walk the same path again, or commit similar negative actions in the future. These imprints must also be removed if we want to fully prevent illness or other negative experiences in this and future lives. We can achieve this by completely purifying the very subtle mind and developing our consciousness, and especially our wisdom through advanced meditation techniques (see appendix 1).

Reiki can greatly enhance our health and protect us from future illness by preventing the potential causes of illness arising from deep within the mind. Illness can only arise from within the mind if other conditions are present; for example, a seed cannot grow into a tree without water, earth, light, and air. Likewise, a potential illness can be prevented from arising by reducing stress, improving our diet, avoiding depressing environments, and most importantly, preventing negative states of mind and poor quality internal energies. The presence of Reiki is a protection against negative minds and impure internal energy. So Reiki works in two ways: it heals existing problems and prevents future ones from arising.

The Space Between

We can compare the mind to a glass of sparkling water. The constant stream of bubbles floating to the surface are like our thoughts and feelings. It appears that we are these thoughts and emotions that arise from within, as if they make up our identity and character, or as if they are the "real me." Our true nature is more like the water itself than the bubbles that arise in it, our essence, in reality, is closer to the *space* between our thoughts and feelings, or simply the lack of "I."

Through the practice of Reiki, all our continually distracting thoughts and emotions subside and we are brought closer to the true nature of the mind. Beyond this sense of deep peace we can eventually experience our true nature or infinite, clear, light consciousness. There is a tangible sense of relief as we touch on these experiences, as if we have returned from a long journey—a sense of coming home. It is possible to bring this deep, peaceful wholeness and clarity into the rest of our daily activities to enrich all areas of our lives. In fact, by understanding and experiencing the true nature of the mind, we can solve all our problems! Reiki can take us along this path to a very advanced level of awareness. If we want to solve all our present and future problems and help others in the best possible way by following the path to full enlightenment, then we can use Reiki to help us study and practice under the guidance of a fully realized meditation master (see appendix 1).

After practicing Reiki for a while, directly after or during the attunements, you may become aware of the presence of Reiki within or around you. This is a very pleasant experience. Someone described it as "feeling like God putting his arms around you." Sometimes it may feel like a gentle "rain" or a humming or vibrating field of energy surrounding you. We should try to encourage these experiences through prayer, meditation, or regular self-treatment. They are a real sign that we are receiving healing and becoming more energetically aware, and definitely moving in the right direction.

However, if you don't get these experiences regularly, don't worry, developing a little more heartfelt compassion and the wish to help others is actually of more value. Of course we are all different and everyone experiences Reiki in different ways according to what we need. Although becoming energetically aware enables us to bring Reiki through consciously and more swiftly—whenever we need it—the most important thing is that we take our time and enjoy Reiki in our own way. The best way to judge your progress is very simple. Regularly take a little time to review your life and look back on where or who you were a few months ago. Try to recall how you felt about yourself and the world around you. If you feel more contented, peaceful, and fulfilled, you are moving on! If you have developed a little less "self" awareness and a little more "other" awareness, you are really moving on!

Transcending and Reiki Sleep

We may sometimes experience Reiki Sleep during self-treatment, or when we receive Reiki from others. It's like a short period of deep sleep; we transcend our normal surface level of consciousness, and a more subtle level of mind arises. It may only last for a few minutes but because we become so deeply relaxed and transcend normal awareness, it can seem like we have been asleep for hours. This can happen in reverse sometimes when one hours' worth of self-treatment can seem like a few minutes! When we regain consciousness from Reiki Sleep we often feel completely refreshed, like we've had a full night's sleep.

These experiences indicate that measured time is not as concrete as it normally appears to be, and that the mind—at source—exists beyond the boundaries of time and space. Indeed, the mind is, in essence, timeless and boundless. Some Buddhist texts define the true nature of consciousness or mind simply as clarity and awareness, like an infinite, clear blue sky or just pure, complete, blissful knowing; a sense of "just being," without any boundaries or definition.

We need deep sleep every night in order to stay in good health. Normally it takes several hours of normal sleep at night before we experience the benefits of deep sleep. Deep sleep and Reiki Sleep are very healing. By returning to the source of our surface consciousness, our subtle mind, we release accumulated physical and mental stress and dip into the pool of pure awareness or clear-light consciousness, which is at the core of our being. Unconscious Reiki Sleep tends to happen more frequently to people who have less regular deep sleep or those who particularly need deep healing.

It's not easy for most people to consciously experience Reiki Sleep. Since our minds are used to operating on a surface level, we do not have the conscious capacity or concentration to stay awake and deeply relax at the same time. This is why we temporarily lose consciousness when we transcend normal awareness and fall into Reiki Sleep, as we do when we fall asleep normally. Dr. Usui was able to manifest, consciously touch and work within the subtle levels of mind because of his many years training in meditation and mindfulness.

As our Reiki practice progresses, we will increasingly experience the more subtle levels of mind both during formal treatment and in our day-to-day life. These gentle, lucid, clear, and deeply happy minds will begin to arise quite naturally from within, and we can, of course, enhance or deepen our experience and understanding of this process through meditation and appropriate study.

The Path of Life-long Learning

Sometimes we may feel that we are not making much progress with our Reiki practice, or perhaps Reiki isn't working for us in the way we expected it would. Whatever path of personal growth or spiritual discipline we choose, we will sometimes encounter difficulties, challenges, and adventures! No path worth walking is without its obstacles and opportunities. Reiki is no different.

If we are looking for an easy ride for the wrong reasons we will be disappointed. We cannot use Reiki to escape or hide from problems or to manipulate the external world as we wish. Reiki is a path of life-long learning and not a guarantee of overnight miracles. We need to use Reiki with patience and wisdom. We can transform adversity if we are willing to transform ourselves as well or instead of our external problems. The more we are willing to help ourselves in this way, the more effectively Reiki will work for us. For some people these skills are almost second nature and can be learned quite easily. For most of us, though, it will take time to develop them through experience. Reiki will help us to find our own consistent middle way, somewhere between our current limitations and potential, and in time, if we are patient and consistent, we will gain great wisdom and skill at using Reiki to transform adversity in to the path to inner happiness. The path of self-healing can be very challenging to practice. We need to have the courage to let go of much of who we think we are, and be open and willing to experience ourselves in a new light. We need a "light" mind to do this; one that is flexible, adaptable, balanced, and capable of creatively transforming our old selves into someone worth living with!

The process of Reiki is one of gently stripping back, purifying, and healing our layers of mistaken awareness, confusion, and false identity and allowing our true nature to gradually and naturally arise from within. Steadily we will become clearer, stronger, and healthier beings on all levels. Enjoying our own personal growth process is very important. The sense of self-empowerment we experience will help us work in closer harmony and partnership with Reiki toward a common goal. This, in turn, will also create greater understanding and experience of our own path and where it is leading. For those who are willing to take this next step in the evolution of humanity there is a world of infinite and wonderful possibilities waiting.

Hand Positions for Head

Figure 5.1 Eyes

With your fingers and thumbs together place your palms lightly over your eyes, so you can see no light if you open your eyes. Do not touch your eyes or restrict breathing by pressing on your nose.

Figure 5.2 Temples

In this position your palms should be over your temples, with your fingers and thumbs pointing toward the crown of your head.

Figure 5.3
Base of Skull

Slide your hands to the base of your skull to the occipital bone (bony lump). Your hands can overlap or stay side-by-side in this position as long as the occipital bone is covered.

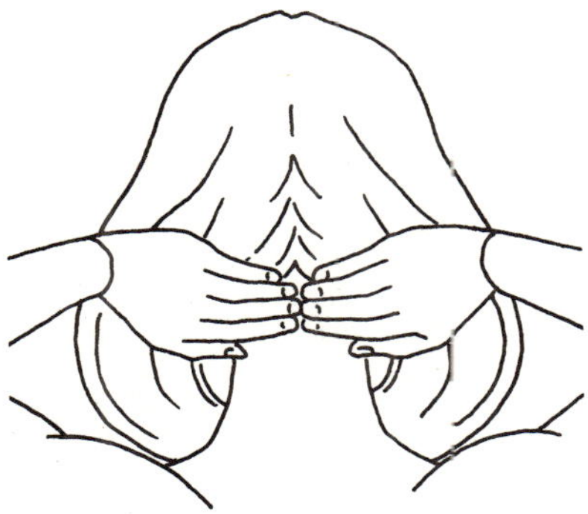

Figure 5.4 Neck and Throat

Bring your hands down to your neck so the base of each palm or wrist touches your throat and the rest of your palms and fingers wrap gently around your neck.

Hand Positions for Front of Body

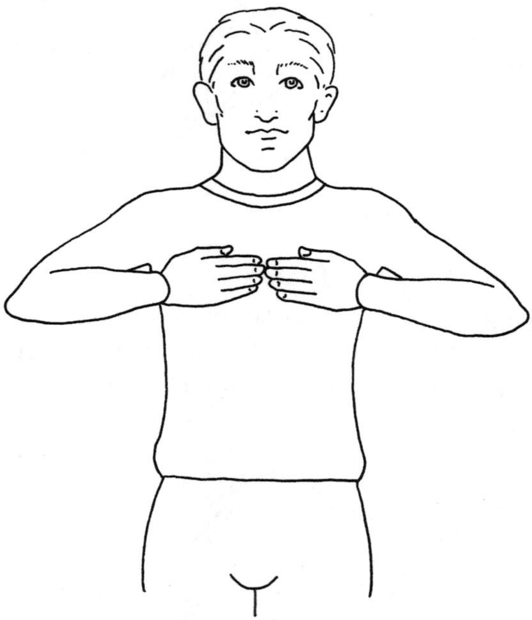

Figure 5.5 Heart

Slide the hands down to the top of the chest, about the level of the heart, so that they are horizontally flat against your chest. The fingertips of each hand should touch lightly.

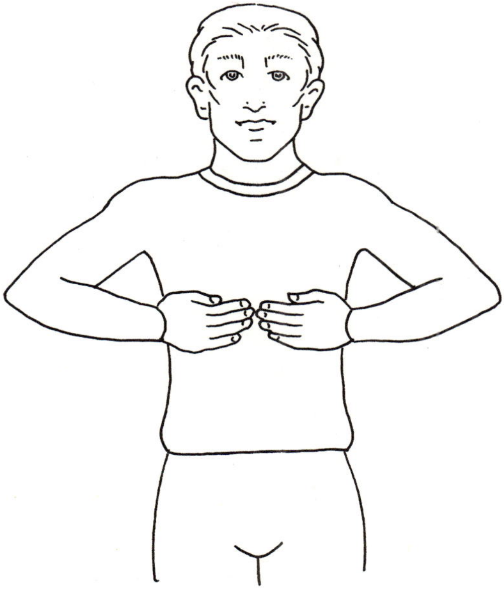

Figure 5.6 Solar Plexus

Again, keeping contact with the body, move your hands down so that your palms rest on the bottom of your rib-cage and your fingers meet directly over the solar plexus, which is directly below the center of your ribcage.

Figure 5.7 Navel

In this position your fingertips should touch gently about an inch below the navel, with your hands still horizontal, if it is comfortable.

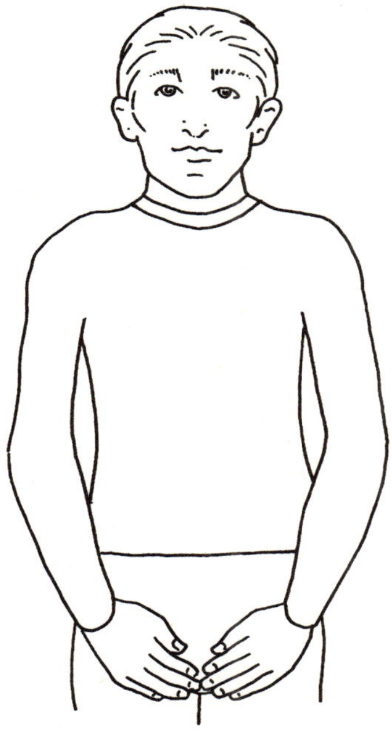

Figure 5.8 Groin

Move your hands down so that they fit into the natural V-shape in the groin. Your fingertips should just touch.

Hand Positions for Back of Body

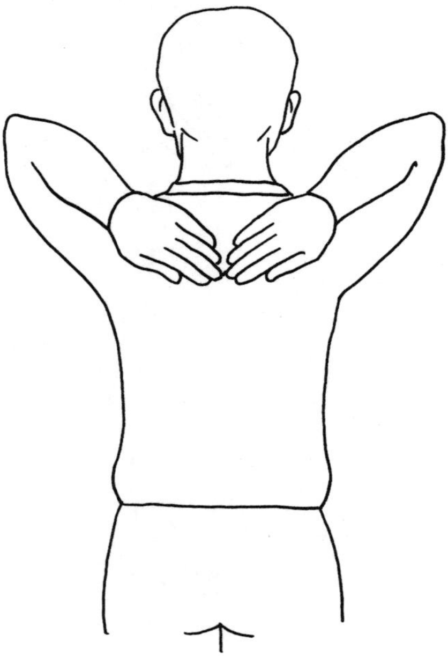

Figure 5.9 Top of Shoulders

Slide your hands up the front of the body without losing contact, and round your neck so that your fingers touch the spine. As far down the back as possible, your hands will form a V-shape.

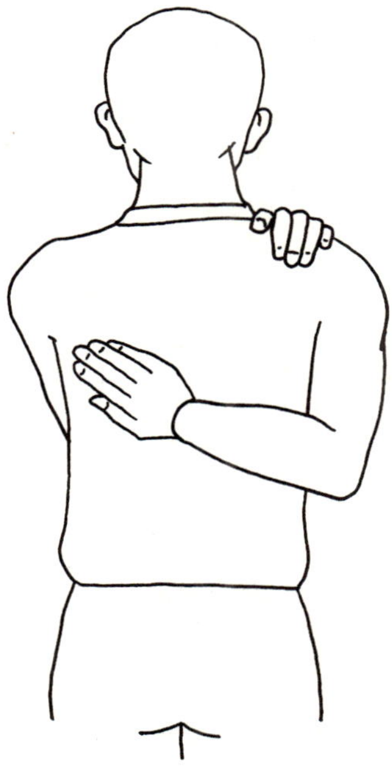

Figure 5.10 Below Shoulder Blades

A. Bring your right hand to the top of your left shoulder and move the left hand so that your palm is flat against the base of your right shoulder blade.

B. As above, but reversed. If you cannot manage this, repeat the front position (see Figure 5.6, Solar Plexus).

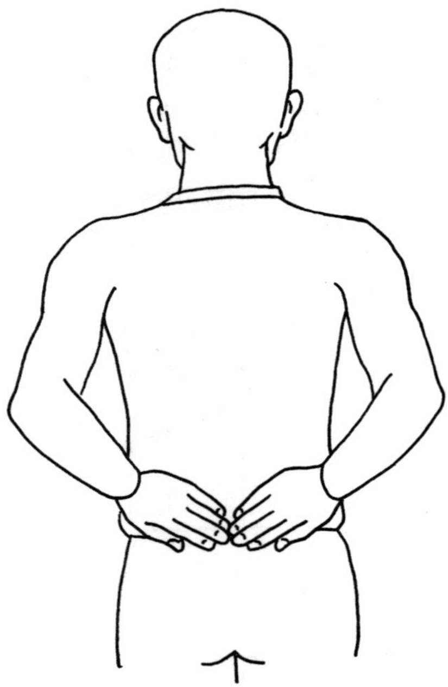

Figure 5.11 Small of Back

In this position, your hands should be at about the level of your navel as horizontal as possible.

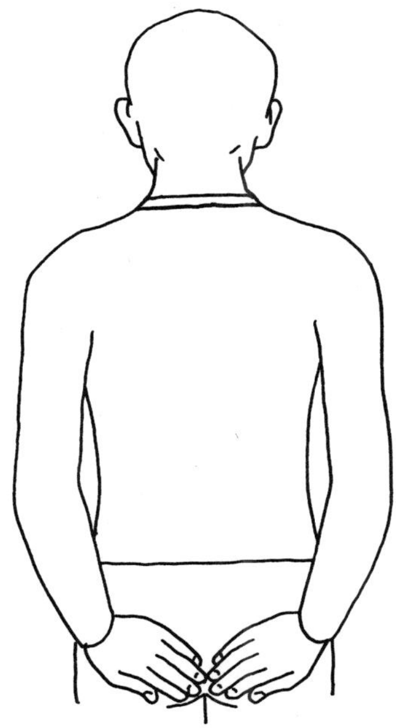

Figure 5.12 Coccyx—Base of Spine

Slide your hands down so that your fingers touch and are level with the tip of your tailbone.

6 Treating Others

Preparing to give a Reiki treatment to another person is similar to self-treatment. Some extras may be needed,[such as a couch or chair, an Aromatherapy burner, low lighting, and a warm room (especially in winter) can be helpful to create the right conditions. If treating someone for the first time, put yourself in their position: how did you feel when you first came to Reiki? Try to make them as welcome and comfortable as possible, without becoming "over-bearing." Allow them time to explain why they have come to see you, and what they expect from the treatment.

Dealing with Client Expectations

It may be helpful to tell your client what to expect during a treatment, however, judge every situation as you think best. Sometimes it may not seem appropriate as they may then be thinking about what might happen instead of just relaxing. Here are some examples of what you may wish to tell your client, if it feels like the right thing to do:

- How long the treatment takes
- Demonstrate the twelve basic hand positions, and explain that you may incorporate extra ones
- Let the client know when it is time to turn over (after the eighth hand position)
- Explain that he or she may experience warmth in and around the body or coming from the healer's hands (occasionally it may feel cool, too)
- Tingling sensations in and around the client's body
- A sense of heaviness or lightness
- Very relaxed, or even sleepy (it's fine to fall asleep)
- The client may talk
- The client may sweat slightly (or twitch), and he or she may feel some movement within the body while relaxing
- Throat may become dry, so have a glass of water handy, and tissues for a runny nose
- Stomach may "gurgle" as the body relaxes

Explain that these are all natural reactions. Some people may have a much deeper and more profound experience or emotional release, so keep a box of tissues at hand, and be ready to listen if needed. Try to be open and accept whatever arises. Trust that your client will know consciously or subconsciously what they are ready to release. The more genuine trust and confidence we have in others' natural healing abilities, the easier it will be for those qualities to naturally arise within them. From the practitioner's side, developing trust in Reiki is part of our *own* healing and growth. It also creates an atmosphere of confidence conducive to ripening your client's own self-healing potential.

If your hands are cold, warm them before starting treatment. This is especially important for the head positions. The first four positions can feel particularly claustrophobic, so be aware that some people may feel uncomfortable about being touched. A Reiki treatment is just as effective if the hands are placed just over the body—rather than touching—however, we know that the power of touch can be very healing in itself, even without Reiki. The question of touch is a particularly sensitive issue when men are treating women, so clearly establish what the client feels comfortable with before the treatment begins, so they can fully relax and receive the maximum benefit of Reiki. If in doubt, don't touch.

Explaining Reiki to Your Client

Sometimes it can be difficult to explain exactly what Reiki is. If your client asks, try to keep your answers simple and honest. The results of the treatment are more important than an intellectual explanation, although talking about Reiki and sharing ideas can be part of the healing process. It can definitely help people broaden their views and look at life from a fresh perspective.

Try to avoid directly challenging people's beliefs, especially if they seem rigid. If they need to change the way they experience and perceive the world, Reiki will help them; it is not our responsibility to guide people as we think fit. Remember Reiki is not allied to a particular religion, it's here for everyone regardless of religious or cultural background. You don't have to believe anything to benefit from Reiki.

Occasionally we meet people that we feel uncomfortable with—and some that we just don't like! If you are faced with this situation with a Reiki client, it will not affect the quality of Reiki they receive, but *will* obviously affect the quality of the client–therapist relationship. Try to be like a good doctor and develop a warm and friendly professional relationship equally with all your patients. Another approach is to use the situation to discover more about yourself. Ask yourself: "Why do I not like this person?" "What is this situation telling me about myself?"

Often the people and situations that we find difficult to deal with are reflections of some part of our *own* mind that we do not fully understand, like a missing piece of the jigsaw puzzle. This is also the case with people we are deeply attached to, or depend upon for our happiness and peace of mind. Most of our relationships are tainted with aspects of need or aversion. Often we need the approval or simply the presence of others to feel secure, happy, and whole, and it is easy to think of many things we dislike or disapprove of in others. We don't have to be completely self-sufficient and separate or completely reliant on others for our well-being. There *is* a middle way. We can give and receive without needing others to feel whole, or pushing others away to feel "free." Pursuing this way of living is a path toward meaningful relationships and personal freedom. This sense of equanimity is also a good attribute to develop and apply to all areas of our lives. If we try to cultivate a balanced, warm, and friendly attitude toward everyone we meet, all our relationships will naturally become harmonious.

Introducing Intent to the Treatment

After the first or second treatment, if you the think the client would understand, you can explain how to set a Reiki "intent" before the treatment begins, and how they can use it to help themselves and their family or friends. This can also be an opportunity for the client to consider the possibility of an inner cause and solution to their problem, and how to address and work with these ideas, so enhancing the extent to which Reiki can help them. However, it's worth remembering that this interactive process is quite natural and should not be pushed or forced. Reiki will probably cause it to arise quite spontaneously, if the time is right.

Before or during the treatment you can set your own intents for yourself, the person you are treating, or others. Don't limit yourself. Use your imagination; send Reiki wherever you want to for whatever purpose. If you want to keep it simple (and simple is often most effective), use one of the following intents, or something similar, that you feel comfortable with:

May every living being benefit
from this Reiki treatment

May this Reiki treatment be for the greatest good

May I be a pure Reiki channel and may this person
receive all that they need for their greatest good

Scanning the Aura

Once the client is ready, it is possible to "scan the aura" around the body to assess areas that may need more Reiki. The aura is a field of subtle life-force energy that surrounds the body of every living being and every other object that possesses life-force energy, such as trees, flowers, crystals, and the Earth itself.

Aura is Latin for "breeze" or "breath." Some Buddhist texts refer to life-force energy as "Subtle Wind." "Gross Wind" is the air turbulence we feel on a windy day. The Oxford English dictionary defines aura as a "subtle emanation, atmosphere diffused by or attending a person, in a mystical or spiritualistic use as a definite envelope of body or spirit." Some "sensitive" and energetically aware people are able to directly see the colors, shapes, and textures of auras and use this ability to diagnose mental and emotional energy imbalances before they manifest as a physical complaint. Also Kirlian photography, which is now well known, actually enables us to physically photograph auras. There are many excellent books available covering auras, energy fields, and chakras, but again detailed knowledge of this field is not necessary to become an accomplished Reiki healer.

To scan the aura, simply place your hands palms down above your client's body and run them slowly from head to feet. You should be able to feel a gentle "cushion" of energy above the body. You can sense this by slowly raising and lowering your hands until just touching the surface of the energy field. It may take a little practice before you can notice this easily. It's important to be relaxed and "open" to sense energy. You can also practice on your own body. With your fingers and thumbs together, move your hands together and apart. After a while, you should be able to feel the energy cushion between them. If not, try stimulating the palm chakras by gently massaging them in a circular motion or vigorously rubbing your hands together. Try this on the rest of your body, especially the areas around the chakras. After some time you may be able to sense your own and others' chakras; some may seem sluggish and some overactive. If you sense an imbalance, give Reiki to that area (see Figure 6.1 below).

It is not essential to scan the aura before a treatment, as Reiki will naturally be concentrated in those areas of body and mind that need it most. If you think the person you are going to treat may think it strange and feel uncomfortable, then don't do it or only introduce it after the first two or three treatments.

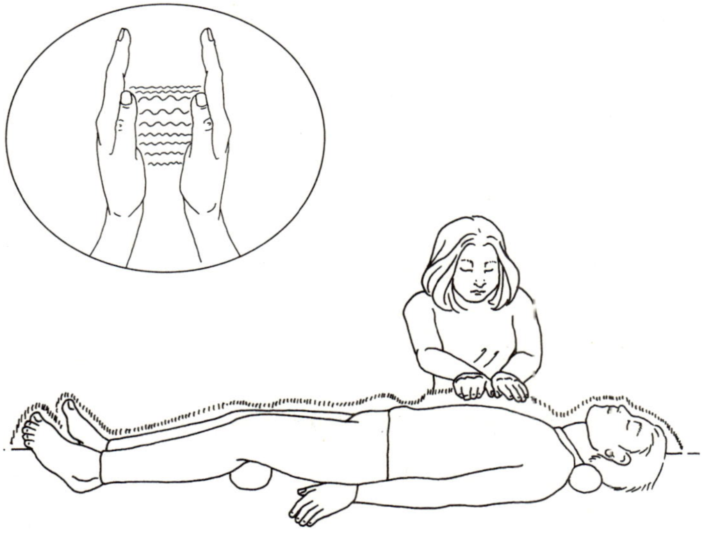

Figure 6.1 Scanning the aura; feeling the aura (inset)

Healing Energetic Imbalances

As you scan down the body, if the energy field dips or rises excessively, or feels cold, hot, empty, or seems to be vigorously vibrating, this is a good sign that extra Reiki would be helpful in those areas. However, this does not usually indicate that there is some physical problem present, so it isn't necessary to mention this energy field imbalance to the client. If you don't know them well, it can sometimes just cause undue worry.

An energy field imbalance may just be a manifestation of mental or emotional stress, recent or from the past, that has not had chance to heal. It's much easier for Reiki to help the person heal and release these problems while they exist on a mental and emotional level. In time, these problems—if not addressed—may manifest on the physical level, however, we cannot be sure when or to what extent.

If you think there maybe a serious, undetected physical problem, try not to alarm your client. Gently encourage them to see their own doctor, especially if they also feel something is not right. Also, they should never be afraid to see another doctor for a second opinion about their current medical condition. If you are a professional complementary therapist, all your clients seeking help for serious medical complaints should come to you after or while they are being treated by their own medical doctor.

Creating an Open Channel

Reiki flows quite naturally as soon as we have the intention to give or when we place our hands on or near the client's body. This is always a pleasant experience and still feels unique, new, and special after years of practicing Reiki.

After the first and second treatments with the same person, you may notice Reiki flowing more freely and strongly. This may be due to your client feeling more relaxed or that problems are being addressed, resolved, and released. When giving Reiki, we should aim to be a clear channel for the energy. This will happen quite naturally once we have taken First Degree. Reiki will always work for the greatest good, however there are some things we can do if we want to take a more interactive role or we feel the energy should be flowing more freely:

- Consume less meat, alcohol, caffeine, and cigarettes if you use them, perhaps just for a few weeks at first to see if it makes a difference for you
- Learn to meditate a little every day
- Take regular, light exercise like walking, swimming, Yoga, Tai Chi, etc.
- Set a clear, honest intent for the greatest good before the treatment, and say/think a short prayer if you wish
- Keep a relaxed and open body and mind during the treatment
- Try not to mentally control or direct Reiki, other than your original intent, unless you are familiar with Second Degree Reiki or similar healing techniques. Keep things simple, and let Reiki do the work
- Trust that Reiki will go to where it is most needed, physically, mentally, and emotionally
- Remember regular self-treatment and receiving Reiki from others is important

- Try not to expect the results that you want, be patient, and enjoy but don't get too attached to good results!
- At the end of every treatment remember to briefly dedicate or direct the future effects of your good karma (positive actions) to some good cause!

If you can keep these points in mind, not only will the results of your treatments be positive and long-lasting, but you will gain great personal benefit from treating others. Your capacity to channel Reiki will continually improve as will your wisdom, compassion, and energy.

Intuitive Healing Wisdom

Given the right conditions, everyone has the natural ability to heal themselves. In some ways, being a Reiki practitioner gives us the ability to provide these healing conditions when others cannot initially help themselves. The presence of Reiki actually encourages or nurtures our own—and others'—intuitive healing wisdom. The less we interfere with this process the better. Too much good-intentioned advice can confuse people who may be already trying to deal with a difficult illness and changes in lifestyle. We don't always know what is best for others!

Often we want to give what others do not need, and trying to provide answers for others can lessen their ability to resolve their own issues. With Reiki, the practitioner to some extent can step back from being a solver of problems and become more of an enabler or simply a "healing witness." This allows people to draw through the Reiki channel what they *actually need* to help them transform their own situation either physically, mentally, or emotionally.

This sustainable healing allows people to develop the qualities they either consciously or subconsciously need to help themselves. It also provides them with skills to deal with similar problems in the future. This can be a slow process at first, but gradually healing the *inner problems* lays the foundation for a deep and lasting overall healing—more than worth a little extra time and effort.

Being a Reiki channel can at first seem unnerving, and you may ask yourself, "What, actually, *is* my job, and *how* do I do it?" With a little experience, you can gain great confidence in the process of letting go to the wisdom of Reiki and to the real needs of your client, without "getting in the way" of that developing relationship. If you do this, you will always be working for the greatest good. Each treatment will take you closer to becoming a more open and complete human being, and therefore more able to help others. *This* is your job!

Completing the Treatment

With experience, you will know when to try new positions that intuitively feel right. Although the legs and feet are not covered by the twelve basic positions, it is good practice to spend another five minutes bringing the energy down to the knees and feet. Experiment and find a comfortable way to do this for yourself. We know that the feet are a doorway to the whole body and treating them through Reflexology and Reiki can have profoundly beneficial effects on the body and mind.

It is important that the Reiki practitioner is relaxed and comfortable while giving a treatment. If the client is lying down, sit on a chair beside him or her while doing the first four or five positions and the feet. It should be possible to rest your arms and elbows on the end of the couch, treatment table, bed, or whatever your client is using. If you want to stay seated, use an office chair on wheels to move around the client's body, but don't rest the weight of your arms on your client's body. Most practitioners prefer to stand up while treating the client.

As in self-treatment it is important not to break contact with the body while changing hand positions. Keep your fingers and thumbs together throughout the treatment. After the eighth position, you will have to ask your client to slowly turn over. If he or she has fallen asleep, gently touch the shoulder, this is usually enough to awaken them. Physically helping your client to turn over allows you to keep contact with the body—important for keeping continuous treatment, as well as preventing your client from falling off the treatment couch if they are sleepy! If the client has a pillow under the knees, remove it at this point and allow them to become comfortable again before continuing the treatment. The treatment usually finishes on the feet, but in some cases a couple of minutes of Reiki on the head, especially the forehead, can help bring clarity to a sleepy mind. This is also a good opportunity to "dedicate" while Reiki is still flowing.

Cleansing the Aura

When the treatment is finished, you can "brush" the aura to remove any negative energy that may have been released during the treatment. This is similar to scanning the aura but instead of the palms being flat, they should alternate between pointing towards the feet as you brush the aura (displacing negative energy) and being flat as you bring your hands back. Slowly work in a repetitive wave motion from the head to the feet, with your hands just below the level of the energy field but not touching the body (see Figure 6.2 below).

When you arrive at the feet you should gently throw your hands toward the ground, thereby releasing the accumulated negative energy from the aura. Set a brief intent for Reiki to cleanse it, so that it does not build up in the room after several treatments. The Life Force Energy of certain types of crystals, including amethyst, have an energy-cleansing effect on the rooms they are in. These crystals themselves can also be cleansed after prolonged use. In fact, the whole area of crystal healing is fascinating and there are many excellent books available on the subject.

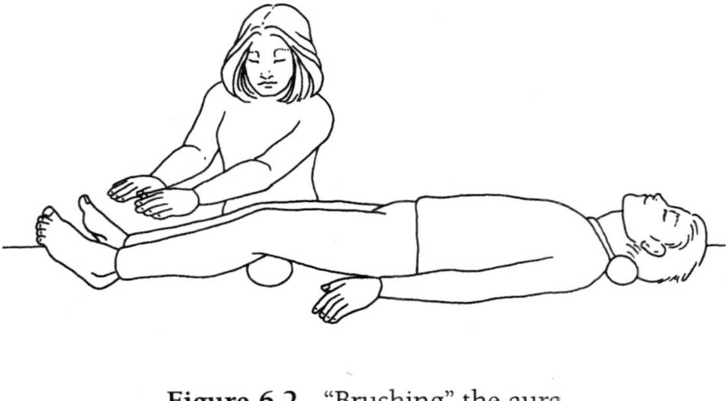

Figure 6.2 "Brushing" the aura

Creating Sacred Space

It is good practice to wash your hands after treatments, helping clear any remaining negative energy. Again, you can touch the client's shoulder if they are not aware that the treatment is over, and tell them to sit up slowly, when they are ready, and then stand up slowly. Give the client time to talk and collect themselves after the treatment. Have water and something to eat handy (such as a cookie), as a little sugar and liquid can help people become "grounded" and alert after a very relaxing treatment. This is especially important if they have to drive home.

If you are doing several successive treatments, give yourself a few minutes Reiki between each treatment and set a mental Reiki intent for the room to be cleansed. This allows time for the energy to clear your own aura of anything you or the previous client may have released during the treatment. It also creates fresh or "sacred" space, for the next person, and it gives you a little time to rest and stay grounded. Giving a lot of Reiki is not usually tiring, but it can accelerate your own transformational process, and this can leave you feeling a little disoriented.

So if you feel this is happening and it may happen at other times, not just when you are giving Reiki, you can either let go, trust and flow with the experience, or set an intent to slow down if you feel things are moving too fast. You always have the choice and the power to decide when, how far, and how fast to progress. Remember Reiki will only ever bring what we are ready to deal with and learn from. Although initially you may not feel up to the challenge, you are always stronger than you believe. If you have a little courage to face self-doubt, Reiki will definitely support you all the way. However, don't create stress, find your own pace, and don't push yourself to change dramatically if you don't feel ready. You can always walk much farther than you can run. Look for balanced, sustainable growth.

Giving Reiki While Seated

Usually it's better to receive Reiki lying down, as this allows a deeper level of relaxation and therefore we can more openly receive healing. However, some people may be

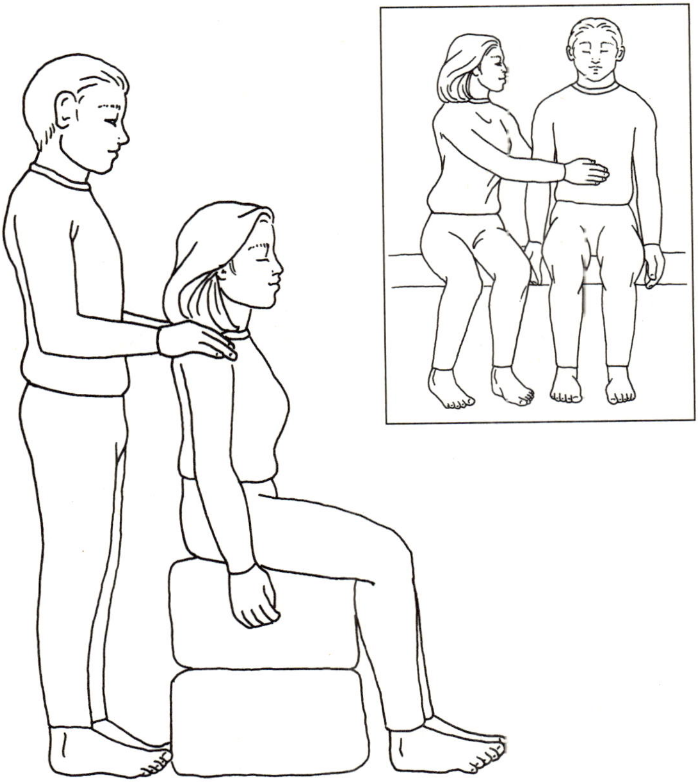

Figure 6.3 Giving Reiki to seated client

more comfortable receiving Reiki sitting up, particularly if they feel vulnerable lying down, or if they have some physical condition such as a back problem (see Figure 6.3, previous page). Assess each case and allow the client to dictate which position they feel most comfortable with. If you give Reiki to someone in a sitting position, cover all the twelve positions, but adapt them so that you and your client are comfortable throughout the treatment. Don't worry if you can't cover them exactly. Reiki will naturally go to where it's most needed.

If your client is seated, stand behind him or her, or to one side for the first four or five positions, then as you move down the client's body, you may sit. It is most comfortable to have one hand on the front and one on the back of the body. Reiki will go right through the chair back as it does with plaster casts, clothing, and other physical barriers. However, if you can work out a way to stay in contact with the body, then this is preferable. Do ten minutes on each of the remaining positions, because you are treating the front and back positions at the same time. Remember that from your client's point of view, sitting for an hour in one position can be very uncomfortable. It may be wiser to use half-hour treatments instead. In the right circumstances, these can be just as effective.

Dedicating After Treatments

At the end of a Reiki treatment, before you dedicate, you can set a further mental intention to seal, protect, and even continue the healing process. For example:

May this person continue to receive as much Reiki as he or she needs until the next treatment

or,

May the effects of this Reiki treatment
be sealed and protected from any
negative mental or physical influences

This ensures that the effects of the treatment continue and last for much longer than the time you have spent with that person.

Always remember to dedicate the positive potential energy you have created by giving Reiki. Do this for yourself, your client, and anyone else you want to help. The karma or actions of giving and receiving healing creates an especially strong potential energy that, as already explained, will return to us as a positive experience some time in the future. Dedicate or direct this energy for specific purposes, or generally for the benefit of all. To dedicate, simply think:

Through the force of this positive energy
may we, and all living beings,
experience lasting health and happiness,

or,

May this act of giving benefit all living beings
for their greatest good.

In this way, a single Reiki treatment can start a positive chain reaction that indirectly helps all living beings, like dropping a pebble in a pool of water. The ripples eventually spread over the whole surface and then finally return to the center or source of the first ripple.

The Power of Reiki Listening

We know that Reiki's natural healing intelligence works in complete harmony with other therapies, often without our noticing its subtle interventions. It helps us develop our own intuitive wisdom so we can become more empathic and aware of how we can best help others.

For example, sometimes we may be aware that a formal Reiki treatment may be inappropriate, and that simply listening to someone talk about their situation is the best way we can act as a Reiki channel. The act of listening is a form of giving. We give our attention with the wish to help, and this creates an "energetic" connection that allows Reiki to easily flow through us to the person in need, aura-to-aura so to speak. The act of asking for help creates an opening, allowing Reiki to enter our client's lives in whatever way they need it.

This "energetic bridge" can also happen over the phone, and even without verbal communication! With some experience, we may begin to notice, sense, or feel when someone is receiving Reiki through us without our conscious intention or physical touch. Since the very purpose of Reiki is to relieve suffering, whenever there is a need for healing and an opportunity or opening to give, Reiki will begin to flow from us, or through us. This might happen anywhere, when we sit or stand next to someone we don't know, when shopping, while waiting for a bus, or just walking down the street. We may also find this happening with people who say they don't want Reiki!

Whenever this type of spontaneous Reiki healing action occurs it is a very pleasant and natural experience, so just relax, trust, and enjoy it. We may also experience this happening with some buildings, places, or other inanimate objects that need Reiki especially if they are connected to some past negative human activities or difficulties, like battles, riots, crime, or traffic accidents. When we experience this happening we can set an intent and dedicate afterwards, however, it is a good idea not to get too mentally involved. We can learn a lot by simply opening to the experience and just being with Reiki.

Healing Past Events with Reiki

Events that occurred long ago may also need Reiki. You can help just by being in these places. Reiki can work beyond the framework of time and space to heal, dispel, and transmute negative energy and the remaining atmosphere of past negative actions or experiences.

If we find ourselves in a place that needs Reiki, we will feel it begin to flow through us quite naturally. If you are comfortable with whatever you are sensing or experiencing then stay with it until it is completed. If not, then just walk away and set an intent for that place or past situation to receive whatever Reiki it needs for the greatest good. That will be enough.

When to Give Reiki

Healing other people and places is like healing a part of ourselves. It accelerates our own personal growth and learning process. If you feel ready to give Reiki on a regular basis, set an intent to attract those people you can help the most. If people don't approach you, then it probably isn't the right time. Maybe you need to spend more time on your own development or perhaps it may not be your path to practice Reiki on a formal basis. Try using your talents and abilities in other areas in conjunction with Reiki. Reiki works in harmony with our lives when we take First Degree. We don't have to make big changes as Reiki will naturally bring out the best in us whatever our other interests might be. Just be yourself!

It's not a good idea to offer Reiki if you think people may be unreceptive or even derisory. Don't be secretive; let people know what you do if it comes up naturally in conversation, and allow them to approach you "if and when" they are ready for treatment. Reiki is a very rare and precious gift and we need to value and treat it with respect. Reiki is here for everyone to benefit from, however, just as we would keep something of great importance to us in a safe place and only show it to those who would appreciate or need it, so it is with Reiki.

If you adopt this attitude of quietness and respect, you will definitely gain greater understanding and experience of the essence of Reiki. It is also worth considering that those living a simple ordinary life as a normal part of a family or community often make for the most profound and quietly effective Reiki practitioners. Being an overtly successful healer, or having a large sense of self-importance as a Reiki practitioner can create many inner and outer obstacles to your spiritual progression.

Glimpsing Our True Inner Nature

Understanding the intimate sacredness of Reiki is part of becoming a more complete practitioner. Sometimes, as we progress, we experience a "closeness within" to the source of Reiki, and at these moments realize we are very small and know very little about the essence of Reiki. However, just as a drop of rainwater is the same nature as the ocean, and eventually becomes inseparable from it, so we realize we are becoming much more than we ever imagined; we can glimpse our own and others' true inner nature and potential.

There is usually a strong connection between the problems people bring to us as healers, and our own issues. If we seem to be attracting people with similar problems, this is an indication that we may need to move forward in these areas too. We can't expect other people to change for the better if we are not prepared to challenge our own shortcomings!

We don't have to be perfect, just prepared to learn more about ourselves. We should never be proud of being a healer, or act in a superior way. This can be a real barrier to our own healing, and to improving our own healing abilities. If we're honest about our weaknesses, without being hard on ourselves, and if we are able to share our problems and ask for help when we need it, then our own ability to heal ourselves and others will improve.

Healing at a Distance

With First Degree Reiki, we can send Reiki to people who need it simply by visualizing them cupped in the palms of our hands, or with our hands on that part of their body that may need particular healing. Just set a mental intent for that person to receive as much Reiki as they need. Sometimes holding a photograph with their name written on the back can help create a stronger connection with the client.

This also applies to distant situations we feel need healing energy, for example, wars, disasters, or other problems we hear about or see in the news. We may meet someone briefly or see someone on the street who really needs help, so again we can send them Reiki in the same way (see Reiki Visualization section, chapter 9, page 171).

Going into Professional Practice

A basic knowledge of anatomy, physiology, and common illnesses can be very helpful if you treat people regularly. If you intend to practice professionally, it can be difficult to get professional indemnity insurance unless you have completed a recognized course of study in anatomy and physiology. Most colleges of further education run such courses. If you are already qualified and practicing a complementary therapy, simply send your insurance company a copy of your First Degree certificate and they will extend your policy to cover Reiki, often at no extra cost.

It can also be invaluable to study basic courses in client care and especially counseling skills. There are many excellent books available on these and other subjects, such as the role of other complementary therapies, self-help techniques for improving health, the mind-body connection, and the way different cultures look at the cause and cure of disease.

The Cause and Cure of Illness

Some people may not always get what they want from a Reiki treatment, or what we would like them to receive! Reiki only works for the greatest good of the practitioner and the client, and this also applies to the results of treatment. The cause of all illness has its root in the mind, and therein also lies the cure of all illness. If the mind is not ready or willing to change, consciously or subconsciously, the illness will not be cured, or we may only achieve temporary relief.

It appears that everyone has the wish to be healthy, however, very few people know themselves well enough to recognize that their illness is an expression of some part of their own mind that does not wish to be healthy, or that does not know how to be well. We can "re-teach" ourselves to be well if we are willing to look within for the answers, and not hand over the responsibility for our health to others.

Reiki works on all levels, but first on a mental and emotional one. Don't be surprised if a physical condition does not disappear overnight. Reiki works to achieve long-term improvements by helping the person address, heal, and release the issues that initially caused the problem. This may happen consciously, or in a very subtle way. Sometimes just learning to accept and live with a major illness is all we can help people achieve, depending on the severity and duration of the problem. We should never regard this as failure. If their quality of life has improved only a little we should be pleased with this progress.

How long and how frequently we treat someone depends on how much they need and how much time we are prepared to give. For a serious condition, it's suggested that we give five treatments the first week, four the second week, and so on until once a week, or until there are no signs of the original problem. Obviously this is not always practical, so once or twice a week to begin with is usually enough, especially as Reiki continues to work long after the treatment has finished.

Mental and Emotional Healing

During a treatment traumatic past events or very happy memories may be recalled by your client as part of the healing process. Although these may seem unrelated to the illness we are treating, they may be very relevant. These recollections can just appear as pictures in the mind—almost like watching a film—which can easily be acknowledged, accepted, and released. There is often no need to analyze or emotionally relive these events unless the recipient has a strong wish to. Again, trust that they know consciously or subconsciously how they need to be during this time. Its fine to stop the treatment sooner if there is an emotional release, and you could spend the rest of the time just talking and listening over a cup of tea!

Treating Children and Animals with Reiki

We can treat children in the same way as adults, however, unless they are very ill, their attention span, and hence their ability to lie still for a full hour, may be limited. So we can either give them shorter, more frequent treatments or treat them when they are asleep, or seated in their parent's lap. Giving Reiki to a baby by simply holding the baby in your arms is a very special experience.

Obviously if we do not know the child well, a parent or guardian must be present throughout the treatment. It's not surprising that children are usually more naturally understanding and intuitively wise to the way of Reiki, and consequently this trust and openness often brings swifter results.

If you want to treat an animal, simply place your hands on or around them—depending on how big they are! Generally speaking the bigger they are the more they will need! Most animals seem to know how much to receive. Often they will come and lean against you for a while and then leave when they are finished. They may even position themselves so that the part they want treated is under your hands. We can also send animals distant healing.

If an animal is really sick, give them regular treatments and work from the head down to the tail, Reiki will go where it is most needed. Reiki can also help relieve pain and stress. This is particularly important if an animal is dying. A peaceful death is a special gift.

Head Positions for Treating Others

Figure 6.4 Eyes

Sit behind your client's head for the first four positions. Place your hands together over or just touching the face, so that your palms are over the client's eyes, but not restricting breathing through their nose.

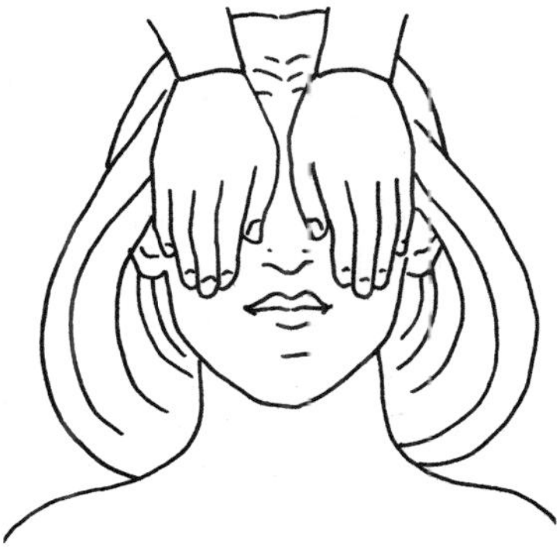

Figure 6.5 Temples

Lightly move your hands to the side of the head so your palms are over the temples and the thumbs touch in the center of the forehead. Alternatively place your palms over the ears and keep your fingers and thumbs together.

Figure 6.6
Base of Skull

Slowly move your client's head to one side so that one hand is carrying the weight of the head while you slide the other hand under the base of the skull. Gently roll the head onto the hand at the base of the skull and slide the free hand around to meet it so that the head is cradled and straight.

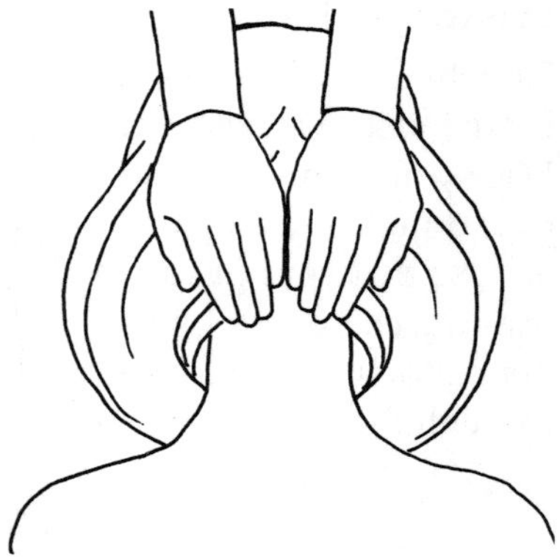

Figure 6.7 Neck and Throat

Reverse the above procedure for removing the hands from Figure 6.6. Bring your hands around to each side of the neck so that your fingers touch over the center of the throat. Your hands should gently touch or be just off the neck and throat.

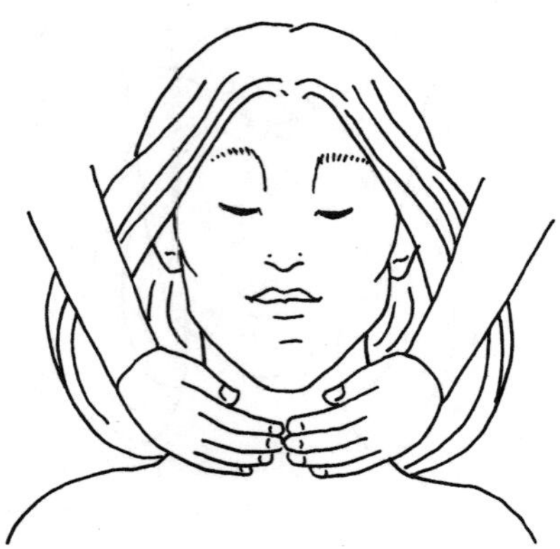

Front Positions for Treating Others

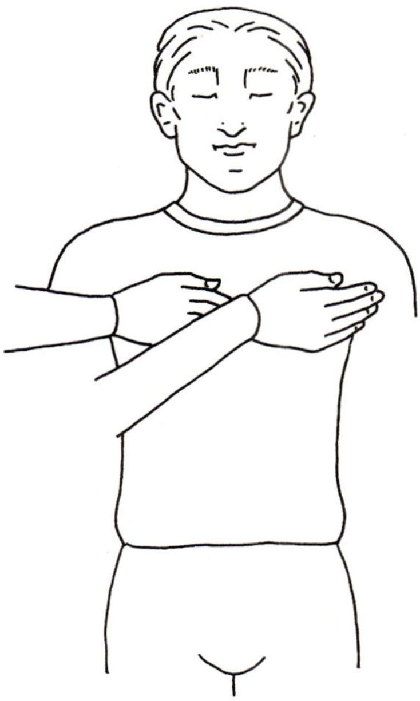

Figure 6.8 Heart

Stand up and move to one side of the client while still retaining some contact with the body. Place your hands one in front of the other across the heart area, so that the fingertips of the nearest hand touch the base of the other palm in the center of the body.

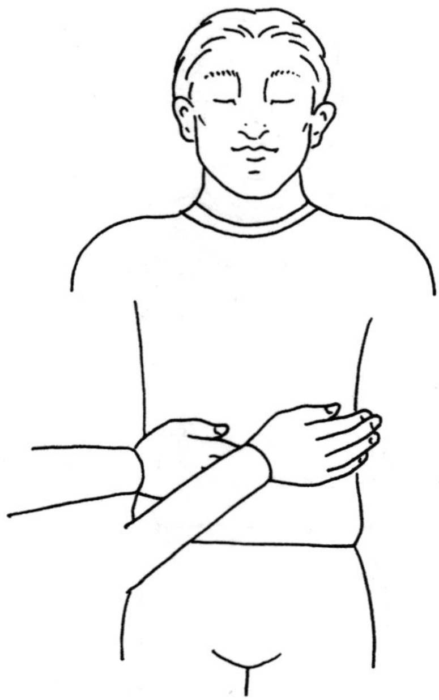

Figure 6.9 Solar Plexus

Move the hands down to the solar plexus area, just below the center of the breastbone. If you are treating a woman, be careful not to touch her breasts as you change position.

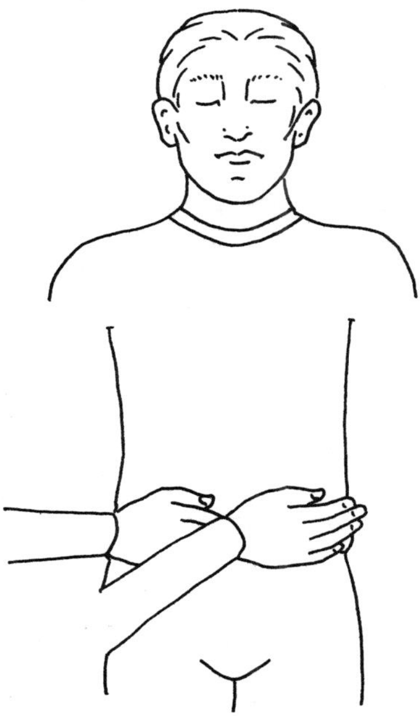

Figure 6.10 Navel
Slide the hands down to just below the navel area.

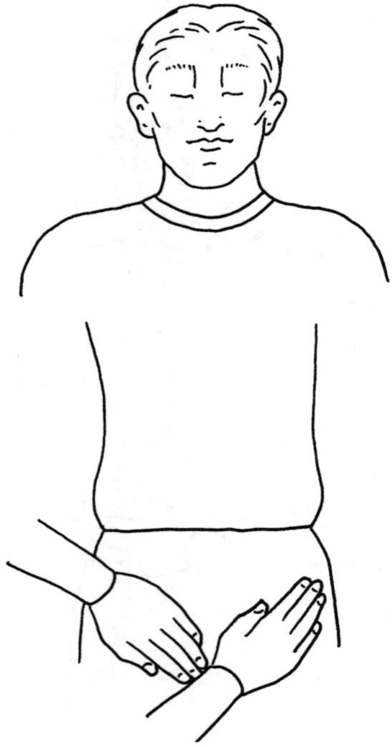

Figure 6.11 Groin

Lift the hands off the body in this position, unless you are treating someone you know well, and position them so that they form a V-shape over the groin area.

Spend a few minutes giving Reiki to the knees and feet before asking the client to slowly turn over.

Back Positions for Treating Others

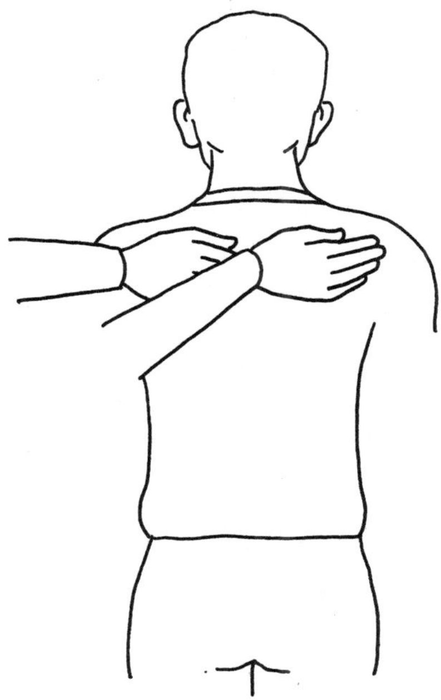

Figure 6.12 Top of Shoulders

Try to retain some contact with the body as the client is turning over and when they are settled bring the hands to the tops of the shoulders so they are in line. Alternatively, you can do this position lower, in line with the heart.

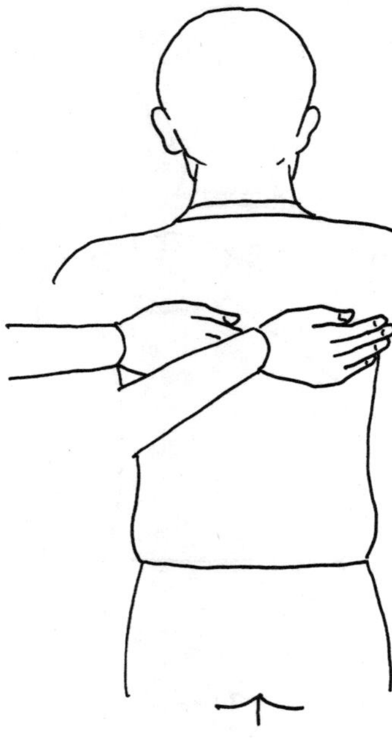

Figure 6.13 Shoulder Blades or Lower

This position corresponds to the solar plexus area, about halfway down the back.

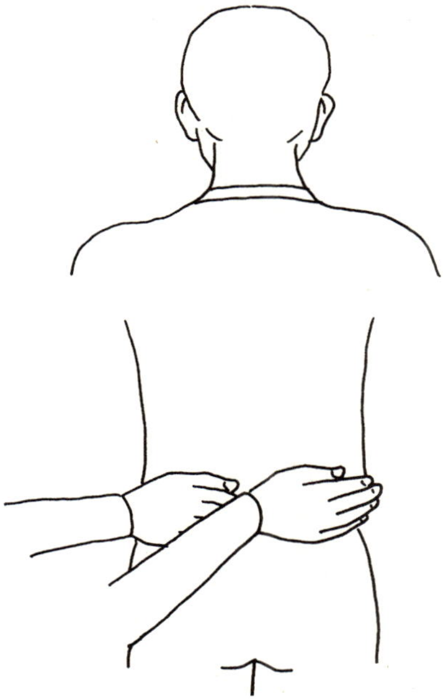

Figure 6.14 Waist

This position should be level with, or just below, the navel at about the waistline.

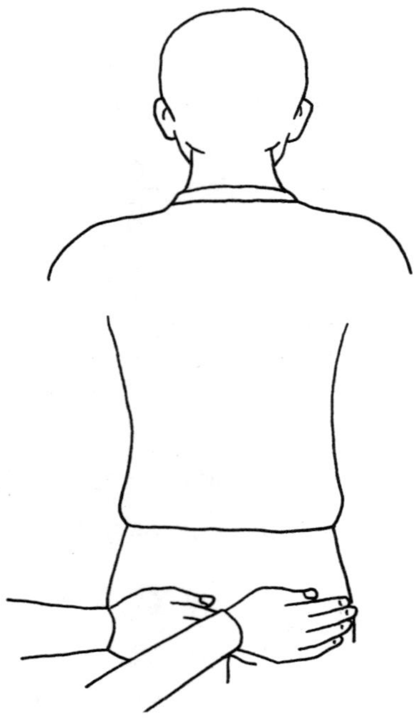

Figure 6.15 Coccyx

Slide your hands down so that they are about level with the end of the tailbone. Only touch this area if you are treating someone you know well.

To finish the treatment spend a few minutes giving Reiki to the client's knees and feet.

7

The Five Principles

Reiki not only heals diseases but also amplifies innate abilities, balances the spirit, makes the body healthy, and ultimately helps us achieve happiness. To teach this to others, you should follow the five principles of the Meiji Emperor and contemplate them in your heart. They should be spoken daily, once in the morning and once in the evening:

> Do not get angry today
> Do not worry today
> Be grateful today
> Work hard today (spiritual practice)
> Be kind to others today

The ultimate goal is to understand the ancient secret method for gaining happiness (Reiki) and thereby discover an all-purpose cure for many ailments. If these principles are followed, you will achieve the great tranquil mind of the ancient sages.

To begin spreading the Reiki system, it is important to start from a place close to you, such as yourself. Don't start from something as abstract or distant as philosophy or logic. Sit still and in silence every morning and every evening, with your hands folded in the "Ghasso" or "Namaste" or also known as the prayer position. Follow the great principles, and be clean and quiet. Work on your heart and do things from the quiet space inside of you. Anyone can access Reiki because it begins within yourself!

An Upward Spiral

To help us gain the most from Reiki, we can use the Five Reiki Principles as a guide to a more involved and responsible personal practice. As explained in Chapter 1, Reiki can improve the quality of our mind, helping us become more positive and creative in all that we do. We know that Reiki does this by purifying and raising the quality of our Internal Life Force Energies, which have a corresponding effect on our thoughts and emotions and the way we experience and perceive the world around us. A good symbolic representation of this interdependent and mutually supportive relationship between consciousness and internal energy might be the Chinese yin–yang symbol or the double-spiral ladder in a strand of DNA.

We can encourage this inner cleansing process by intentionally seeking to create a healthy and positive outlook by practicing the Five Reiki Principles. Regular intentions to develop good attitudes followed by positive actions of body, speech, and mind will actually create clear, strong, and healthy internal energies. This allows you to carry a higher level of Reiki, which in turn deepens the cleansing process and consequently improves and supports our positive mental intentions. We can also see this process as a two-way relationship, through the medium of our internal energies. Our good intentions and the presence of Reiki create a mutually supportive upward spiral towards inner and outer health and well-being.

Regular
Reiki
(Raises quality of internal energy
—creates positive outlook)
+
Positive
Outlook
(Raises quality of internal energy
—improves level of Reiki)
=
Health
Well-Being
(Positive continuous upward spiral)

The Pure Wisdom of the Principles

The importance of the Reiki principles is emphasized in Dr. Usui's memorial inscription. The Meiji Emperor of Japan originally devised the principles as an easily remembered guide to developing and sustaining a relaxed, peaceful, and positive outlook—basically how to live a meaningful and fulfilling life. A truly positive state of mind is one that brings lasting happiness to ourselves and others. If we fully embrace these principles as part of our Reiki practice the wisdom, compassion, and power within them can guide and support us not only in our use of Reiki but in all other aspects of daily life.

The Reiki principles are pure wisdom. Each one carries a special energy or essence. Perhaps Dr. Usui taught them to help us understand the importance of taking responsibility for our own actions and to help us realize our own value and potential by using Reiki *for the greatest good.*

If we use Reiki in accordance with the five principles, our motivation will naturally be correct and the results of our actions will always be for the greatest good. If we adopt the principles, we will live in accordance with the ultimate intention of Reiki: to benefit all living beings. All our Reiki intents will be achieved more swiftly and easily, and all our thoughts and actions will in time become a pure and natural expression of our good intentions.

Although the principles appear simple, they contain the essential teachings from all the great spiritual traditions. If we use Reiki regularly, with a genuine wish to learn more about ourselves and benefit others, these realizations will come naturally.

The Five Reiki Intentions

If you find your health (or other problems) are not improving, and you are giving yourself regular treatments, you will need some space and "quiet time" to find a solution. By using the Five Reiki Principles, you can identify those qualities you need to overcome the difficulties you're facing. This can be quite challenging, but also very rewarding. If you continue to build on your successes, those positive qualities can be a real refuge when your faced with future challenges.

Once we have identified the principles that are most applicable to our situation, we can transform the Five Reiki Principles into the Five Reiki *Intentions:*

Today I am peaceful.
Today I am relaxed.
Today I am grateful.
Today I work hard (meditative/spiritual practice)
Today I am kind to others.

Use the Five Reiki Intentions for issues you're dealing with in the same way you would set and use a normal Reiki intention. If you want to develop a particular intention, it's helpful to meditate on it daily (as explained later in chapter 9, page 180). Also, use the five intentions as "trigger lines." When suddenly faced with a difficult situation that challenges your patience, remember the intention: "Just for today I am peaceful." If you have set this intention and familiarized yourself with it during your regular meditation or Reiki sessions, then simply recalling it will help you stay calm, peaceful, and relaxed.

The Wind of Reiki

Each principle is open to personal interpretation, so when we look at them we need to be honest about our strengths and weaknesses. The principles are not there to restrain or restrict us; in fact, the opposite is true. By following these guidelines we develop increasing inner peace and contentment, and we become able to deal with problems in a positive way. By experiencing the essence of these principles, we live in harmony with the greatest good and this increases our ability to benefit from Reiki.

If we allow Reiki to touch our lives in this way we can begin the upward spiral towards health and well-being. Like a bird, we can learn to use the wind of Reiki to lift us and help us glide effortlessly to our destination, metaphorically speaking! Although there are ancient Buddhist and Vedic scriptures that tell of previous, more openly spiritual ages when it was not uncommon for advanced yogis with very pure internal energies to travel by physically flying when it was necessary. Indeed there are some accounts of famous Christian mystics or saints actually hovering above the ground while they prayed. This shows a clear link between sincere prayer and meditation, our internal energies, and developing spiritual consciousness.

Applying the Five Reiki Principles or Intentions in conjunction with regular Reiki treatments on ourselves and others can help us increase our wisdom, compassion, and inner strength. By trying to develop these three rare and precious qualities we will naturally be living in accordance with the greatest good, the expansion of happiness for all.

Happiness is simply a state of mind. With each principle we are asked to give up a particular negative state of mind that is unhappy, and cultivate happiness in its place. The overall message is quite simple:

Abandon Unhappiness,
Develop Happiness

Developing Mindfulness

Releasing negative habits and learning to develop genuine positive thoughts and feelings about ourselves, our circumstances, and others, is the key to lasting happiness. It takes practice to develop day-to-day mindfulness, to recognize our thoughts, rather than being carried away on the endless stream of worries, distractions, and emotions. Stopping and examining our thinking through the practice of daily mindfulness, meditation, and Reiki are the first steps toward real freedom.

Mindfulness, to some extent, develops effortlessly through regular self-treatment. Our internal energies become more consistently clear and stable, consequently the states of mind that "ride" on those energies become more pure and positive. We become more self-aware and less self-absorbed. Although this process is quite natural and gradual, we can accelerate our progress by *developing mindfulness*. The space and peace this creates in the mind is the foundation upon which we can build lasting happiness by learning to develop and trust our inner resources of wisdom, compassion, and inner strength. If we are serious about wishing to find a lasting solution to life's problems, here is an opportunity! If we want to study and practice this path to completion we need to consult someone who knows it well and teaches it simply and clearly (see appendix 1).

Thoughts on the Five Reiki Intentions/ Principles

It's useful to make notes on how you perceive the meaning of each principle. Keep a journal and regularly update and refer back to it. This deepens and clarifies your awareness, tracks your progress, and highlights possible areas for improvement.

How do you relate to each principle, and what do they communicate to you? Which are particularly challenging and which particular situations or people come to mind with those principles? Regular meditation on a particular principle, and self-treatment with the appropriate Reiki intention, are the best ways to develop the qualities we need to transform our personal issues (see Meditation on the Five Reiki Principles, chapter 9, pages 180–183). Here are some thoughts and ideas on each of the principles that might be useful. Each of the original Reiki principles is followed by the modern Western version in parentheses, and the appropriate Reiki intention in italics.

Don't Get Angry Today (Just for today do not anger)

Reiki intention: *Today I am peaceful*

What is the antidote to anger? Simply, patience. It's easy to see patience as merely an uncomfortable "grit-your-teeth-and-bear-it" state of mind, however, the truly patient mind is able to accept difficult circumstances while remaining peaceful and happy. Depending on your circumstances, this may not seem easy, especially as we so often feel justified in our judgment of others' "wrong" actions. No matter how justified we feel, if we check, anger or irritation is an *uncomfortable* mind. If we have been hurt by someone, why do we hurt ourselves more by feeling the pain of *anger?* We have a choice. Surely common sense tells us to develop the state of mind that will help the hurt heal most easily. If you burn your hand, you immediately put it under *cold* water, not *hot!* Developing anger can only cause more conflict. Patience and understanding can actively *diffuse* confrontation and promote compromise.

Patience does not mean that we should *suppress* anger. This only leads to resentment, bitterness, and related physical illness in the future. Patience and forgiveness are the healing *middle way* between the extremes of either suppressing or indulging anger and other strong negative emotions. The practice of patience is a deeply transforming process. It creates a peaceful and stable mind, and enables us to release negativity as it arises in the mind without losing ourselves in related thoughts and emotions. Patience also gives us the mental space and clarity to judge our responses to challenging situations with wisdom, fairness, and honesty.

Practicing patience means willingly accepting and transforming everyday annoyances or difficulties into the path toward personal happiness and inner contentment. Once on that path we are better able to benefit others. Normally we would avoid any amount of irritation, but with gentle, regular determination, we can use these opportunities to gradually learn to relax, accept, and eventually welcome the chance to practice developing a peaceful mind in "trying" situations. Also we can quickly and directly purify the negative karma (resulting from our previous negative actions) that is causing the unpleasant circumstances to arise and remembering this can help us maintain peaceful patience!

Anger is the most damaging and destructive force known to man. We should be vigilant and never allow ourselves to be controlled by it. When we are under the influence of anger we easily lose control of our thoughts and actions; we say and do things we later regret. Just as a forest fire starts from one small spark, so violent anger can easily develop in a mind that readily becomes frustrated or impatient with small problems. Anger gets us in to trouble and pride keeps us there! Anger is our worst enemy. We should only ever get angry *at* our anger.

Don't Worry Today
(Just for today do not worry)

Reiki intention: *Today I am relaxed*

Has worrying ever solved a problem? Much of our lives are filled with worry: minor day-to-day worries and more deep-seated, long-term anxieties about health, career, and relationships. Many people have had difficult events in their lives and are burdened with pain or guilt. But many of these problems are beyond our immediate control. The future is uncertain and events rarely turn out as we expect. Much of our attention and energy is lost by carrying the *weight* of the past and worrying about a "maybe" future—so much so that we miss the *present!*

By learning to accept the things that have happened to us, however painful, we can release ourselves from the past. By being content with our life as it is, we prevent craving and dissatisfaction in the present, and anxiety about the future. These simple thoughts create a sense of peace and freedom in the mind, and—if deeply felt—allow us to relax and fully enjoy life. A Buddhist teacher once said, "I do not think it is possible to be too relaxed, as long as laziness is not regarded as relaxation!" The more relaxed and content we are the closer we are to our true nature—where not even the smallest "stress" exists.

You may ask yourself if it is necessary to worry about other people's problems. Does this actually *help* them? Or, in fact, on some subtle level, does it actually reduce their ability to *help themselves*? Having genuine confidence in others' abilities to overcome adversity is more beneficial than worry. Of course we can be deeply concerned for the welfare of others, and this will motivate us to assist in whatever ways we can. Concern is a beneficial state of mind leading to active helpfulness. Worry just leads us in negative, self-absorbing circles.

Cultivating Compassion

What is compassion? From a Buddhist perspective compassion is the wish to relieve others' suffering, protect them from future suffering in the wisest way possible, and to act on that wish. This basic wish is our Buddha nature and is the source of many spiritual realizations. Compassion is a wise action of body, speech, or mind that arises out of empathy or understanding of others' problems. It is a very empowering, active, purposeful, and deeply fulfilling state of mind—a long way from worry! In fact we could see compassion as the opposite or antidote to worry.

Worry is an uncomfortable, self-centered, inward looking mind that restricts the free flow of healthy life force energy, bringing more problems in the future. Compassion, on the other hand, is a wide, expansive, happy, giving, and deeply peaceful mind that creates a boundless and effortless flow of positive energy. If we gradually and regularly try to increase our compassion, by contemplating the difficulties and potential dangers that all living beings face, then firmly resolving to help others however we can, eventually we will be able to directly release and protect others from suffering. This is the power of compassion, and the nature of Reiki.

Be Grateful Today
(Show gratitude to every living thing)

Reiki intention: Today I am grateful

Each person sees the external world in a different light. Our environment appears to change depending on our state of mind. If we have an angry mind for some reason, no matter how beautiful our surroundings are, or how kind people are towards us, we will be unhappy. However, if we have a mind of gratitude, then the world appears to be an easier place to live, even if our circumstances are difficult. Of course our external world has not changed but our mind has. Understanding this is the key to lasting happiness.

Developing a sense of gratitude toward others and the world you live in is like developing a real treasure in your own mind. It keeps your mind "light" and positive, and prevents depression and despondency if your external conditions become difficult. A "problem" is just a challenging set of circumstances viewed with a negative mind. If we reduce our ability to become negative by increasing our sense of gratitude, we reduce our problems! Gratitude is a mind of "giving." When we appreciate and value ourselves and our life, we love and appreciate others.

Counting our blessings rather than meditating on our problems creates contentment. Familiarizing our minds with contentment helps us to remain relaxed and at peace with ourselves amidst the changing fortunes of life. Practicing contentment actually cuts at the root of many of our daily problems. Contentment is the antidote to needing those things we are attached to for our happiness and trying to avoid those things we dislike. This is a quiet but very powerful and wise middle way to inner happiness.

Work Hard Today—Spiritual Practice (Earn your living honestly)

Reiki intention: *Today I work hard*

The essential spiritual practice of all religions is developing compassion. There is nothing more positively powerful than compassion guided by wisdom. A wise mind knows that to fulfill our compassionate hopes for the welfare of others, we must realize our own full potential as a spiritual being. If our wish is strong enough and we have the correct conditions, methods, instruction, and guidance we can achieve this within one lifetime. It is said that it is easier to attain full enlightenment in one human lifetime than it is to attain another human rebirth! There is no doubt that we currently have a very rare and special opportunity.

So this principle is mainly stressing the value of life and asking us to assess our priorities before it is too late. We do not know how much time we have left to live; many young people die before their parents. We rarely think about or acknowledge death as a daily possibility. Even on the day we die, we will probably not think: "I may die today, how can I make the most of the time I have left?" So there is no doubt that we are very complacent about death, we all think we will be here tomorrow, but many people will not. All we really have is today, we should remind ourselves of this every morning if we wake up! Perhaps this is why all the Reiki Principles end with the word *today;* awareness of death as a daily possibility really concentrates the mind and helps us see clearly the importance of acting now to change for the better and use our life wisely. Wake up, grasp the value of life before death has you in its grasp. Then when death comes, you will be content and well prepared.

Perhaps we ignore death because it makes us feel uncomfortable or frightened but if we have not prepared ourselves in some way it will be a great shock and a very stressful experience. Then at the time of death we will feel lost and alone, or we will not know what to do or who to turn to for help. Having a sincere daily spiritual practice, enjoying life to the full, and taking refuge in an honest relationship with God, Buddha, Allah, our own higher nature or however we perceive the greatest good, is the best way to lead a meaningful life, and prepare for death and our next life. Dr. Usui knew the importance of this and must have taught it to his students as an integral part of the practice of Reiki.

The Western version of this principle, Earn Your Living Honestly, seems simple on the face of it. Most people appear to earn their living "honestly," but if we look from another perspective, we can see that many people often lack honesty toward themselves and others.

Dr. Usui realized that one of the reasons his initial work with Reiki was only partly unsuccessful was due to a lack of effort or only a weak intention on the part of his students to help themselves. Laziness or not pulling our weight in society, in our family, or in our relationships is "draining" on others and ultimately self-destructive. We need honesty and clarity to see this form of subtle selfishness. Earning your living honestly and living your life with integrity and fairness is an act of giving, especially if this is our conscious intention. Ask yourself a simple question: "Am I a giver, or a taker?" A giver is also able to "receive" from others when in need, rather than "take." Receiving can be an act of giving, if our motivation is to benefit others.

In earning our living or in any other aspect of our lives, if we strive to follow our heart and not the crowd, then we are living honestly and fairly. This may not be the "safest" route and initially we may not get others' support. However, if it is our true path, then many people will benefit from our honesty and courage. We will naturally attract the right conditions for this path to progress successfully, and because we enjoy what we are doing, making an effort to progress will not seem like hard work.

Living our life honestly, and without deception, is a path to truth. Being open and honest about our weaknesses helps us become stronger. When, through honesty, we begin to know our own mind, then we become more able to help others gain the same benefits for themselves. The qualities of honesty, increased self-awareness, and the wish to help others form the foundations toward complete wisdom. Experiencing these realizations will naturally bring us lasting peace and happiness, and enable us to share peace and happiness with others.

Be Kind to Others Today
(Honor your parents, teachers, and elders)

Reiki intention: *Today I am kind to others*

Buddhism teaches that all the good things we experience in life are the result of our wise and kind thoughts, words, and actions toward others in our previous lives. All our negative experiences, even down to the most minor irritations, are the result of our unwise, negative, and selfish actions. You can see how important this principle is. If we put the welfare of others high on our list of priorities, as well as enjoying the short-term sense of fulfillment this brings, we can be sure that our kindness will return to us as some similar good experience in the future. Then we will also find it easier to develop positive, compassionate, and wise minds. If we tend to put our own welfare first we will encounter many inner and outer problems in the future. Of course, being kind to others does not mean we should be unkind to ourselves! Feelings of guilt, worthlessness, and self-pity are as damaging as negative thoughts or actions toward others.

If your attention is regularly and consistently directed toward helping others, you gradually reduce your sense of self-importance, your sense of "I" or ego. This naturally makes you more relaxed, content, peaceful, and happy. Hawayo Takata once said, "No I—Just like that you will find health, happiness, and security." This may seem strange at first, we may think, surely if I reduce my sense of *I* or if there is *No I*, then how can I be happy!

To really understand this apparently conflicting view we need to meditate and study the authentic teachings that Buddha gave on this special method for finding lasting happiness. Briefly though, we can think of it like this: The mind or consciousness has no I, no sense of identity, there is no real me. The true nature of the mind is simply pure clear awareness, cognition, or knowing. The sense of I we experience when we think or feel has no real basis for existence, it is simply a strong habit of conceptual thought and feeling that we take with us and develop from one lifetime to another. We can see this mirage like I more clearly when we are embarrassed, annoyed, ashamed, elated, or ecstatic.

However, if we try hard to look for the I or "real me" in meditation we cannot find it! It is not in the body or the mind and obviously not somewhere else. Also if we can observe, experience, or witness our obvious I, perhaps when we are embarrassed or jealous, how can it be us, the observer? At that time it is just like any other external object that our mind comprehends and as explained earlier all external objects, like all phenomena, no matter how real they appear, are just projections of the mind, like in a dream.

All our selfish negative actions and reactions are motivated by the need to protect or satisfy our strong sense of I. We are always doing things for the benefit of this nonexistent, dream-like apparition of the self. In fact if we think clearly, we will see that all the worst things that mankind has ever done, all the wars, atrocities, and abuse of others, has been done to satisfy the self-centered I. We do not need to worry if we do not accept or understand these lines of reasoning. We only need to see that by reducing our sense of the overly self-important I, by opening our hearts and increasing our regard for others, we will find lasting happiness and fulfillment. Then, if our intention is strong, many fortunate opportunities for us to help others will naturally come our way.

The Western version of this principle, "Honor you parents, teachers, and elders," comes naturally to many people from the East where the wisdom and experience that come with age are highly valued and respected commodities. Often we take the good qualities and kindness of others for granted and concentrate more on their faults. This only leaves us feeling resentment about the past and dissatisfaction with the present. In this frame of mind we are powerless to change anything for the better. Even if we had an unhappy childhood, our parents still created, nurtured, and protected our life every day in the best way they knew how. They gave us shelter, food, clothes, and taught us many important skills that we still need to use daily. Without our parents we would never have been able to learn, practice, and read about Reiki or any other path of healing. Where would we be now without their patience and care?

To honor someone is not to put them on a pedestal, or to lower our own self-esteem. It is to be grateful, to respect, and to recognize their good qualities. Older people have more experience and can teach us so much if we are prepared to listen carefully, and make room for new ideas between our own opinions and pride. Pride can often stop us being open to new growth, if we think we are usually right, then we are usually wrong! Being honest about our faults gives us humility, allowing us to change and grow. Then everyone becomes our teacher, and every situation is an opportunity to learn. We can even regard children and animals as our teachers. Their uncomplicated honesty and natural openness can be a very positive influence.

By honoring and respecting all forms of life, we recognize and therefore indirectly nurture their individual potential to become "all that they can be." In Buddhism it is said that deep within the mind all living beings possess "Buddha Nature"—the potential to attain a fortunate rebirth and work toward full enlightenment for the benefit of all. Again by recognizing, respecting, and encouraging this potential in others, we create the causes for our own good qualities to develop, and eventually become complete.

Infinite Inner Wealth

Practicing the Five Reiki Principles is a true cause of happiness. A true cause of happiness is something that brings more happiness the more we do it, or the more we have of it.

More money, cars, relationships, or whatever—they only bring increased temporary happiness. If this were not true then all rich people would be very happy, and the more wealth they accumulated, the happier they would become! Happiness is simply a state of mind, an inner quality.

Happiness does not depend on external factors, and it does not exist outside of the mind, or separately from it. Although some external factors, like relationships, good food, or music, appear to cause happiness to arise in the mind, we cannot say they are a true source of happiness. If they were, they would always cause us to experience the same level of happiness. We know this is not true. Sometimes when we feel deeply unhappy no manner of external factors can help us feel better. Also we know that sometimes happiness simply arises in the mind for no apparent reason. Sometimes we just feel happy and this shows that we don't necessarily need things to make us happy. By learning to understand and control the deeper levels of our mind we can decide for ourselves how happy we want to be, whatever our external circumstances.

The more we develop our inner happiness by practicing the Reiki principles, or other similar spiritual guidelines and teachings, the more happy and content we will become. We can even take this potentially infinite *inner wealth* with us when we die! Developing our inner qualities in this way is the most powerful and meaningful way to use Reiki.

8

The Nature of Disease

Basically, any disease, disorder, or unhappiness is the result of some disharmony in the body, mind, or environment. However, it's not easy to establish the original cause of a particular problem. After studying Buddhism, Dr. Usui would have understood that the root causes of all our major and minor problems are our own previous negative actions of body, speech, and mind returning to us as illness, poverty, ignorance or any other type of unpleasant experience.

Karma directly translates as "action," or something we intentionally create mentally, verbally, or physically. The laws of Karma teach that whatever we create comes back to us sooner or later—just like a boomerang! These negative actions may have been performed many lifetimes ago and it is only now that we might be experiencing the repercussions. We may think that we would never have committed serious negative actions, like harming others, but in each of our previous lives we were almost completely different from the kind of person we are now. If it were possible to meet ourselves from a previous life, we would not recognize ourselves at all. It would be like meeting a complete stranger.

Buddhism suggests that each lifetime we are almost born anew, on the surface we have completely different bodies and personalities, yet deep within our very subtle mind, soul, or higher self, we carry the memories, tendencies, and imprints of all our previous lives and all the actions of body, speech, and mind that we've performed. When the conditions are right, these actions will return to us as positive or negative experiences depending on whether they were well-intentioned and beneficial or otherwise. From a Buddhist perspective (as explained in chapter 5), to fully heal and prevent future illness we must remove the root causes or "seeds" of our past negative actions from deep within our mind, before they ripen as new unpleasant experiences. If we find these ideas hard to accept, there are other ways to understand the apparent causes of illness.

The Will to Change

We should try not to avoid problems, but seek an understanding of their origin and thereby arrive at a lasting solution. We do not have to accept problems; there are always many things we can do to improve our quality of life, whatever our level of health or wealth. Simply by adopting a peaceful and positive state of mind, we exercise our power to enjoy life. We can achieve this immediately. It doesn't take weeks or months to learn, in every moment we have the power to change our lives forever.

All that you are now is what you have created consciously and subconsciously in response to your circumstances and experiences since the day you were born. With birth, you bring the different general (and specific) mental, emotional, and physical tendencies, along with habits of body, speech, and mind you developed in previous lives. This explains why children in the same family are so individual from the moment of birth, and even while in the womb.

However, even deeply ingrained and apparently natural characteristics are impermanent, and can be changed with an honest and strong intention. This may seem like very simple psychology, but why make it difficult? Whatever your situation or personality, all you need is an intention to change for the better, a willingness to learn, and a happy, relaxed mind!

Reflections of the Mind

Buddha explains the creation of the external physical world as simply a projection or reflection of the mind. The world we inhabit is a mental projection with which we have become so familiar that it appears real, solid, and permanent in almost every way, perhaps like a very vivid and recurring dream that we return to each morning when we wake up! We know from experience that dreams can appear to be very real. For example, in a dream we can touch solid objects, have conversations, go to work, go on vacation, or do anything else that we might do in the real world. These experiences can seem so real to us that we only know that we have been dreaming when we wake up. In a dream we can even ask others, "Is this a dream?" and they might say, "Of course not, don't be silly," as they would in everyday waking life.

When we wake up, where have all these apparently solid objects, environments, vivid experiences, and dream people gone? We know that they never actually existed in the way that they appeared to, they were simply projections of the mind. Most people don't believe that this might also be the case in the real world because it seems so real! This is why it can be such a painful place to live and why we get so attached to the things that seem to afford some relief from the potential for unhappiness that is always present.

By developing our wisdom mind—through meditation, prayer, and Reiki—we can develop the clarity of awareness to pierce the veil of dream-like illusion that is the root of all our problems—including illness. This wrong awareness causes us to perform or create negative actions or karma of body and mind in response to an apparently "real" or important world. When this negative karma "ripens" it keeps us tied to the cycle of ignorance, wrong action, and subsequent unhappiness until we find the rare opportunity to wake up, that is, until we're on an authentic and complete spiritual path.

Subtle Symptoms of Greater Problems

Our bodies, environment, relationships, job, and possessions are like reflections of our gross, subtle, and very subtle mind. Gross objects like everyday solid forms, people, relationships, and environments are like reflections of our gross mind. Subtle objects, like those in dreams, are like reflections of our subtle mind and very subtle objects, that are impossible for most people to perceive, are like reflections of our very subtle mind. We can interpret the subtle and very subtle mind as the subconscious mind or that part of our mind that we cannot consciously control or that we do not clearly know. From early childhood we have been taught to live in response to the external "real" world. We are unfamiliar or generally unaware of our internal nature and the problems and potential therein. We cannot help but project ourselves, our faults, and imperfections onto the outside world. We do this so completely that we have no perception of our true nature.

If you have problems with your health, finances, friendships, or anything else, this is like a bell ringing; a symbolic message that some part of us, internally—either mentally, emotionally, or spiritually—needs attention. This may seem unusual but with experience we can begin to see clearly that our faults or imperfections are constantly being reflected back to us by our bodies, the environment, and our everyday experiences. Most people accept that if, over time, we suppress or overindulge strong negative thoughts or emotions, this can lead to physical or external health problems or harmful addictions. Ask yourself: What am I unhappy about? What problems do I have at the moment? You may be able to trace these outward manifestations back to some aspect of your inner nature that is not fully developed or in harmony with the whole.

For example, when people are lonely they often turn to food, drink, cigarettes, shopping, or superficial relationships. Consequently if we have problems or addictions in these areas, might it be because we are lonely? If we can identify the true mental or emotional cause of the external problem, we are halfway to solving the issue. The other half of the answer is to develop the real desire to change, regain, and rebuild or develop that inner part of us that we have lost or abandoned, and are presently looking to replace with some external comfort or support.

In the case of loneliness we can try to release the need to gain happiness from others or external objects by developing an inner sense of self-acceptance. Contentment and eventually deep peace and joy will follow. This doesn't mean abandoning relationships or other physical pleasures. In fact, releasing the need for these things actually allows us to gain greater enjoyment from them; our relationships become clearer, healthier, and more rewarding. It can take time to release our old habits, to create and feel deep contentment but it can be done if our wish to change becomes consistently stronger than our negative beliefs and habits. Reiki can help us greatly along this inner path.

Other Symbolic Symptoms

On a less obvious level, specific health problems can symbolically relate to specific causes in the mind. For example, we use our shoulders to carry heavy weights. Shoulder problems, therefore, can relate to carrying too much responsibility or not being responsible enough. Also, the neck is very flexible and allows us to look in different directions, so neck problems can relate to rigid thinking, or giving in too easily to others. We use our eyes to see where we are going, so eye problems can be related to not wanting to see things as they really are, or trying too hard to control things. We use our legs to move forward in life, so leg problems can be related to wanting to stay in a particular situation, perhaps because it feels safe or we are striving too hard to achieve the wrong things.

We can apply this line of thinking to any health problem. Just think, "What is this problem telling me about myself?" "What does this issue represent symbolically?" Generally there are two extremes and a healthy middle way. If we sit and think about this quietly and honestly the answer will usually come simply and easily. We know ourselves better than we think! Don't make it complicated; just keep an open mind and remember all the answers are within you. If you don't feel ready or able to change, you don't have to. It's up to you!

We can even apply this wisdom to apparently inanimate objects. For example, if your car battery is dead, do you need more time to rest and recharge? If the front door to your house jams, do you have difficulty letting people into your life, or are you too open and accommodating? If you have a pipe that bursts or a light bulb go out, are you under too much pressure or do you always seek to avoid stressful situations for a quiet life? This may all seem a little "far-fetched" but with practice we can develop the wisdom to see ourselves everywhere and to use every situation as an opportunity to learn about our inner nature through its reflection in the external world. Obviously this way of looking at the world can also tell us what we are doing right! So if we are generally content and attract good conditions or positive relationships, this indicates that we are moving in the right direction.

Dealing with Accumulated Karma

It can be difficult, challenging, and sometimes painful to face the inner root of a problem, especially when it appears that an easier answer or diversion can be found in the external world. However, lasting solutions to our problems can only be gained by going within, by changing and healing the mind. If we can familiarize ourselves with this inner path, we will gradually find our problems diminish. They can be replaced by an awareness of a deep and continuous source of happiness from within. This will naturally make our external world a more pleasant, meaningful, and harmonious place to live.

Sometimes no matter how positive we are, or how hard we try, and no matter how much Reiki we receive or other therapies that we try, we cannot improve our health or resolve other major issues or problems that may be making our life unpleasant. Unfortunately this is a fact of life that we are all aware of. Buddha says that we have had countless previous lives and the amount of karma we have accumulated is nearly boundless. Sometimes some of the effects of our previous negative karma appear so overwhelmingly strong, deep, and persistent that we may not be able to purify them or escape their effects in this lifetime. Being realistic rather than negative about this can help us come to terms and live within our limitations whatever they may be. Also, as mentioned earlier, by accepting whatever misfortune comes our way with a peaceful, positive mind, we can gradually learn to enjoy life more fully and at the same time naturally and swiftly purify our negative karma, therefore eventually gaining freedom from it.

There are some advanced, yet simple, Buddhist meditation practices that can purify even the most negative karma in one lifetime. Seek the teachings, advice, and guidance of a qualified teacher to practice these techniques. (For more information, see appendix 1.)

The Twelve Hand Positions of Reiki

The following is a general guide to the physical, mental, and emotional areas covered by each of the twelve basic Reiki hand positions. A full Reiki treatment will naturally cover all areas of the body and mind and Reiki's natural healing wisdom will concentrate the energy in those areas that are most in need. It is not necessary to remember all of the information relating to each hand position; simply use it as a reference if you want to take a more active role in directing Reiki to where it is most needed.

These guidelines are also useful if you or the person you are treating wish to understand the mental and emotional aspects of a particular illness or problem. If you treat someone else, it might be a good idea to use this information in conjunction with scanning the body (see chapter 6) and, of course, ask your client relevant questions about their condition.

Head Positions

Eyes

Physical: Eyes, brain, pituitary, pineal glands, nose and sinuses. Reduces headaches.

Emotional: Reduces stress, helps one unwind and calms an overactive mind; reduces extreme emotions.

Mental: Improves clarity and quality of thought; attention span and concentration; increases mental energy; helps in decision-making and developing confidence; awakens the "third eye" and improves intuitive inner wisdom.

Temples

Physical: Headaches, seizures, shock, motion sickness; balances left and right brain and hormonal responses, vision and ear problems.

Emotional: Stabilizes fluctuating emotions, reduces worry, and depression; balances male/female aspects of body and mind; opens mind to new ideas, new ways of thinking and being.

Mental: Creates calmness and balance; clears thought processes; improves assimilation and comprehension of information and short-term memory, creativity and spontaneity; opens crown chakra to create a strong link to higher consciousness.

Base of Skull

Physical: Whole nervous system, weight, spine, pain relief, speech problems.

Emotional: Relaxing comforting and nurturing; improves long-term memory and the ability to accept and release past difficulties; relieves depression.

Mental: Deeply relaxing; helps us switch off and release repetitive worries; strengthens body and mind.

Neck and Throat

Physical: Speech problems, jaw, teeth, larynx, thyroid, lymphatic system, balances blood pressure.

Emotional: Reduces or releases suppressed thoughts and emotions; improves confidence; releases tension; improves ability to communicate and be honest and open.

Mental: Brings calmness and clarity of thought; flexible thinking and the ability to see all around you and look for new horizons; creates an open and clear mind.

Front Positions

Heart

Physical: Heart, lungs, thymus, immune system and circulation, asthma and other bronchial disorders.

Emotional: Relieves stress and increases confidence and courage and the ability to feel love, joy and compassion.

Mental: Thinking becomes less selfish and more motivated by the wish to benefit others.

Solar Plexus

Physical: Liver and gall bladder, stomach, spleen, digestion, pancreas, nervous system, diabetes.

Emotional: Releases fear and aggression; improves power of self-expression and self-determination, and the ability to accept and feel strong emotions without being overwhelmed.

Mental: Balances thinking; becomes more centered and less easily influenced or diverted or distracted.

Navel

Physical: Abdomen, intestines, colon, bladder, food allergies.

Emotional: Balances sexual feelings, guilt, attraction, obsession, repulsion.

Mental: Improves ability to "digest" new ideas and to think clearly without being distracted by strong emotions.

Groin

Physical: Lymphatic system, urinary system, intestines, male/female sexual organs, constipation, diarrhea, hips.

Emotional: Sense of security/safety; sexual pleasure; releasing strong emotions and repetitive or offensive behavior.

Mental: Improves energy, vitality and self-awareness and alertness; will to survive and living life to the fullest.

Back Positions (similar to front)

Shoulders

Physical: Lower neck and shoulders, heart and lungs, upper spine, neck injuries.

Emotional: Releases heavy emotional and mental burdens and issues that have been ignored.

Mental: Helps to clear the mind of mental and emotional baggage and face issues or problems from the past.

Solar Plexus

Physical: Kidneys, adrenals, lower lungs, pancreas, stomach, spleen, midspine.

Emotional: Improves physical and psychological strength and releases burdens and past emotional trauma.

Mental: Improves mental stability and power of thought.

Lower Back

Physical: Intestines, bladder, lower spine.

Emotional: Similar to above and front position; also improves ability to relax; feel and express strong emotions and enjoy balanced sexual expression with love and without guilt.

Mental: Improves acceptance, expression and understanding of strong emotions.

Base of Spine

Physical: Lower back, hips, prostate, male/female reproductive system.

Emotional: Releasing old patterns of behavior; making room for new ideas or ways of being; releasing built-up emotion or improving ability to easily experience then release emotional responses.

Mental: Increases mental power and ability to react positively, creatively and instinctively in difficult or emergency situations.

The areas covered by the hand positions listed above are a general guide built up from experience and common sense. If you feel drawn to treating a particular area without a logical reason, then follow your intuition. Nine times out of ten you will get results and each time you do your intuitive wisdom will improve.

However, never think that such intuition or guidelines like the ones above are grounds for making a medical diagnosis or for treating a condition without the correct conventional medical treatment. Always check that the person you treat has seen a doctor if they need to. If a Reiki client refuses to consult a doctor, it is best to stop treating them until a correct medical diagnosis is established.

9

Reiki Meditation

We can direct Reiki for any specific purpose. Or, we can simply allow Reiki to work for our greatest good by just relaxing, trusting, and allowing the presence of Reiki to permeate our life. Alternatively we can find a balance by consciously setting Reiki intentions, while being open to the wisdom and guidance of Reiki. In this way we will learn from experience how best to use Reiki, how to develop a closer more open relationship with Reiki, and gradually establish the way we want to be as a practitioner *living* Reiki.

We can use some of the following techniques to help us deepen our Reiki practice, learn to relax more easily, and create positive states of mind which in turn will benefit all those we come into contact with, especially if that is our conscious intention.

Enjoying Reiki Relaxation

This can be done either sitting up or laying down, and combined with some—or all—of the twelve Reiki positions. Relaxing music maybe helpful. If you only have fifteen or twenty minutes, choose one head position, one front position, and one back position, perhaps the back of the head, heart area, and lower back, groin, or leg area.

Begin by making a conscious Reiki intent to completely relax your body and mind, and to receive whatever healing you need during the time you have available. Also take a moment to set specific intents for yourself and others. Take a few deep breaths and settle into a comfortable position. Let go of anything that might be on your mind. This is your time to relax, and it's important that nothing distracts you.

Bring your attention to your toes and try to "find" any tension there and release it. At first it may be helpful to tense and then release them. You need to gradually familiarize yourself with the experience of consciously relaxing, then the process will become easier. Move your attention slowly into the rest of your feet, consciously relaxing each part. If it helps, you can think "release and relax" as you slowly bring your attention to the ankles, shins, calves, knees, etc. Continue to move your attention up through the body, consciously relaxing each part. If your attention wanders simply return to the last location.

When you have reached the top of your head spend a few minutes being aware of how it feels to be completely relaxed. The more you remember this experience, the easier it will become to repeat and use in your daily activities. This technique can take some time to master, so don't be disappointed if you still feel some tension after the first few sessions. This will pass in time and the technique will become more natural. At this point you can stop, dedicate your positive energy, and get up slowly, or continue with a simple visualization.

Using Reiki Visualization

Visualize a spiraling stream of golden or white light entering through the crown of your head and filling every part of your body. Try to move the light slowly down, so you get a sensation that each part of your body and every cell is filled with "light" energy. We can then imagine that our whole body and mind melt into this light, which slowly expands to fill the room, the house, town and country, the whole planet, and finally the whole of space. Spend time enjoying this experience of clear light filling the whole of space.

This is a good point to think of others who may need healing, local or world conflicts, disasters, or simply every living being. Visualize these people or situations surrounded by the light and imagine that all their problems or sickness are easily transformed and healed. Continue to visualize them as healthy, happy, and content for a few minutes. We can think and try to really believe how wonderful these people are now, actually free from their pain and problems. Then concentrate for as long as possible on the feeling of joy that arises from this thought. Don't worry if at first this feels false or manufactured. With consistent and sincere practice, your motivation will become more natural and powerful. Also, don't try too hard or make your visualizations too complicated; an *honest intention* and a strong belief that your positive thoughts have really helped are the most important aspects.

The power of the mind is limitless. By strongly imagining that through our actions people are released from their problems, this creates the causes for it to actually happen in the future. When you have finished, visualize the light coming slowly back into the space of your body and seal it in with a mental intention such as:

Balanced, centered, grounded,
blessed, and protected.

Then get up slowly when you are ready, and dedicate the positive energy you have created. Sometimes when we are setting intentions like the one above or dedicating the positive energy created through a Reiki action, it may helpful to say or think the intention three times. This sets the intention firmly in our minds and helps us to see if the intention sounds or feels "right." It may be too complicated, or not clear enough. We can change an intention simply by saying or thinking a new one that applies to the same person or situation, for this will automatically override the previous one, if it is for the greatest good! The power of our intentions and dedications are dependent upon the sincerity and stability of our true heart-felt wishes. So we need to keep an eye on them and check them regularly!

Sitting with Reiki

Once attuned to Reiki, you will gradually become more aware of its presence in your life. You may experience this as a sensation of inner peace and wholeness, or as a "cushion" or a presence of energy and love surrounding your body, or a flow of energy through you. Sometimes you may feel it automatically "turn on" or come through more strongly, as either you or the people around you need it. We become a kind of gateway or channel for the healing energy to help others.

When you feel Reiki coming through more strongly, it is a good idea to find five or ten minutes for a "Reiki break."

Sit with it, soak it up, and give it out, but obviously only if it is convenient. If this happens and you feel the energy concentrating in a certain area of your body or particular thoughts and emotions arise regarding some problem you have, try to relax and allow Reiki to work for you. Just "watch" your body and mind and don't get too involved with whatever feelings, thoughts, or sensations arise. Just allow them to flow through you and release in whatever way feels balanced, clear, and natural.

If you can open up and trust in this way, answers to problems will simply arise or the issue will pass more quickly than if you had tried to mentally "solve it" or emotionally overindulge it. This natural releasing and healing process can work for any stressful situations that we are dealing with. Even past events from long ago, that have not been fully accepted or healed physically, mentally, or emotionally, can be healed. With a little practice you'll be surprised at how quickly Reiki can resolve problems and change the situation for the benefit of everyone involved.

Developing Inner Peace

The process of watching your mind or developing mindfulness is also a very powerful way of developing inner peace and natural intuitive wisdom. A good time to practice this is during self-treatment, or when you treat others. Simply look for the moments of natural peace and stay with them. When distractions arise in your mind or body, or you are disturbed by a noise, don't worry or become irritated or involved. Simply witness or watch these small events and allow them to come and go, continue watching your mind and body and the peace will return sooner or later.

Follow this inner peace and try to naturally stay with it without straining the mind, so that you become more and more familiar with it. In time this experience will arise more easily and naturally, and you will not need to consciously find or stay with it. Eventually this natural inner peace will become your normal state of mind and as you continue this practice you will gain deeper and more profound levels of self-awareness and happiness. You may find it helpful to try this practice while treating yourself sitting in a chair, as it easy to fall asleep when laying down. Also, using hand positions that cause muscle aches may cause unwanted distraction. In both cases, see what feels right and works for you.

A Quick Lift

We can also learn to "turn on" Reiki when we need it. This is a great way of regularly "plugging in" to Reiki and can be very useful when we don't have time to treat ourselves fully but need a quick lift.

Simply sit down, put your hands somewhere comfortable (like the top of your thighs), and set a mental intent to open your body and mind to Reiki and receive all that you need. Allow yourself to fully relax and go with whatever experience comes to you. If you can spend ten or fifteen minutes doing this every day, you will definitely experience positive results.

This also helps to increase our awareness and understanding of Reiki and it teaches us how to open and bring Reiki through more swiftly and consciously when we need it. We also become more able to control and gauge our reactions to situations rather than being victims to impulsive negative thoughts, emotions and actions.

This method is also useful if we have a specific problem or issue that we want to resolve. Before you begin, simply bring the issue to mind and set a clear intent to find a solution for the greatest good. Then relax, enjoy the Reiki, and see what arises in your mind. Sometimes an answer may come hours or days after the self-treatment and might be sparked off by reading something relevant to your issue, meeting someone, or some other type of useful "coincidence!"

Reiki Mantra Meditations

We can use the word Reiki as a mantra. A mantra is a special word or group of words that, when spoken or thought, have a positive effect on the mind and body. The word "Reiki" is very blessed and if used as a mantra—with Reiki healing energy—can enhance our abilities to give and receive healing. We can use it with the "Sitting with Reiki" meditation, or when we are giving or receiving Reiki.

Simply allow the word "Reiki" to arise in the mind effortlessly and naturally, like a spontaneous thought. We should not force it to arise, just allow it to surface easily like a bubble in a glass of water. When it does arise, follow it, listen to it, repeat slowly or more quickly—just listen to it, feel it, and follow it. If your mind wanders off, just bring your attention back to the mantra and continue to follow it. This can help you develop a closer relationship with Reiki. It takes you closer to the source of Reiki, and therefore closer to your own true nature. You can use other special words in the same way; words like peace, compassion, wisdom, Buddha, Jesus, Divine Mother, Holy Father, or groups of words like, "whole, healthy, and happy," "completely relaxed and peaceful," "strong, confident, and clear." Use any of the Five Reiki Principles or Intentions in a similar way.

We can also meditate on the deeper meaning of Reiki by asking: "What is Universal Life Force Energy?" "Where does it come from, outside ourselves or from within us?" We can ask Reiki directly for a clearer understanding of our own true nature or for answers to specific problems we may be facing. It is up to us how far we want to go, and how much we want to know. Reiki will only bring us what we are ready to cope with and able to understand.

Using Buddhist Mantras

There are many mantras used in Buddhism to heal, purify, and help develop certain positive qualities of mind. The word mantra means "mind protection." Mantra appears as words or sound, although the Buddhist Sutras or Holy Scriptures tell us that in reality mantra is *Life Force Energy.* Therefore we could say that Reiki *is* mantra. One of the most well-known mantras is OM MANE PADME HUM, roughly translated, these Sanskrit letters mean "all praise to the jewel in the lotus," although they have deep meaning on many levels. The jewel in the lotus refers to our Buddha nature or greatest potential for good arising from the lotus, which is the symbol of compassion. The mind of compassion, or the wish to develop compassion, is the source of our greatest potential and worthy of the highest praise.

OM MANE PADME HUM is the mantra of compassion and has a profound effect on the heart chakra, bringing great inner peace and contentment. We can use this mantra at any time or we can receive a special empowerment from a Buddhist Geshe (Master) and combine the mantra with an especially powerful but simple form of meditation practice to develop our compassion and ripen our potential for benefiting others. For this mantra, we need the empowerment of Buddha Avalokiteshvara, the Buddha of Compassion. Buddha Avalokiteshvara had such a great wish to help others that he blessed his own name so that when anyone one said it three times they would receive relief from fear. This is still a very effective way to prevent and relieve fear, in any situation.

Say or think the mantras when you receive Reiki from or give Reiki to others. If our intentions are truly compassionate, this is an especially powerful action or karma as the nature of mantra is so pure, holy, and blessed. Our level of compassion directly affects our ability to heal others. Say mantras for others whenever they need help, perhaps for people who are distressed, sick, and homeless, even for dying animals or insects, this will help them greatly. Then we can also dedicate the future effects of our actions or karma for their benefit. This is a special form of giving and will greatly increase the power of the karma that returns to us in the future.

To develop our wisdom, we would need to receive the empowerment and the mantra of Buddha Manjushri, the Wisdom Buddha. To develop our healing abilities we would need to receive the empowerment of Medicine Buddha ("Sange Menhla" in Tibetan, see Figure 9.1, next page), the embodiment of all the Buddha's healing qualities.

Regarding Mikao Usui's quest for Reiki, we know that he must have used Buddhist methods for developing compassion, wisdom, and healing abilities on his path toward Reiki. (If you wish to know more about these techniques or practice them yourself, see appendix 1.) Buddha's teachings are widely available to people of all religious and cultural backgrounds, and as with Reiki you don't have to be Buddhist to benefit from them.

If we decide to practice mantra recitation without receiving an authentic Buddhist empowerment and learning the appropriate meditation practice, then a sincere intention and dedication for the greatest good can really empower and protect our practice.

Figure 9.1 Medicine Buddha
(Used with kind permission of Andy Weber, Tharpa Publications ©1990)

The Earth Healing Meditation

This is a very simple and enjoyable meditation to do. It is especially effective if you can do it outside, perhaps in a garden or in the countryside, if it is warm. Also, it is more powerful if you find a tree to rest your back against while doing it, as trees can act as a junction for the energy exchange. Do this meditation either sitting up, standing, or laying down, and for as little or as long as you want.

There is a natural exchange of External Life Force Energy between a tree, the Earth, and the Universe. In some oriental philosophies, trees are seen as symbolic or actual gateways between heaven and earth, with their roots soaking up nutrients from the Earth and their leaves stretching towards the light of the sun and the energy that it gives. They are also seen as an example of how we should approach life. Growing steadily year by year a tree is strong yet balanced and able to change with the seasons. It bends and does not break in high winds because its roots are deep, and the tree is flexible and adaptable to the forces of nature. When the conditions are right—as in summer—its growth rate increases accordingly, and in winter it rests and recharges. Likewise, we can only be effective spiritual beings if our feet are firmly planted on the ground, and we know when it is time to challenge ourselves and time to rest.

Choose a tree that you feel drawn to, and place your back against it, with your feet or backside between two roots, if they show above ground. Take a few moments to get comfortable and "tune in" to your surroundings, then close your eyes and slowly relax your body and mind. Set an intent to give Reiki to the Earth and to all the living beings on Earth for their greatest good. Then imagine Reiki in the aspect of white or golden light spiralling through your crown chakra and filling your body and mind until you feel completely peaceful and relaxed. Then visualize Reiki entering the Earth through your base chakra or feet and descending directly to the center of the Earth. From there the energy radiates throughout the whole planet, then our solar system, the whole universe, and all worlds and realms of existence. The Earth and all living beings are released from all their problems and blessed with Reiki, the nature of love, compassion, and wisdom. Then the main emphasis of this practice is to concentrate on the feeling of joy that arises from believing that we have directly helped others. Try to let your mind merge with an ocean of loving joy. We can stay with this experience for as long as we wish, before slowly bringing our attention back to where we are sitting. This universal healing is a very powerful and compassionate act. Then, as always, we can dedicate our good karma and, if we wish, protect our own energy system by thinking and feeling:

I am fully blessed and protected by Reiki.

Meditations on the Five Reiki Principles

Reiki works well with all types of meditation and relaxation techniques. Whatever technique you use, simply set a mental intent before you start, such as:

May Reiki help me gain the greatest benefit from this meditation.

This improves your concentration, clarity, and experience of meditation. It helps carry forward your positive intentions into the rest of the day. The effects of regular meditation combined with Reiki can greatly improve your quality of life.

We can meditate on all five principles, or just those that we feel are most appropriate for our situation. If we have a particular problem, we can choose the principle that we feel may hold the answer and meditate on it until we are ready to move on. Meditating on one principle a day, in five-day cycles, is a great way to continually improve your wisdom and compassion, as each meditation builds on the previous one and each cycle takes you a little closer to wholeness and happiness: the source of Reiki.

Prepare for meditation by finding a regular, daily, quiet time—about fifteen to twenty minutes or more. Early morning is often best, when you are fresh. This can really help you start and continue your day in a positive way.

The room should be peaceful and clean, and if you have a particular religious belief, set up a small shrine or altar as a focus point. This also serves to hold the spiritual energy in the room and house—which is symbolic of your own body and mind. Clean and look after this space regularly, and treat it with respect. This will definitely cause your meditations to gradually become clearer and deeper with long-lasting effects. By inviting the universal blessings or greatest good in to your house and life by creating a small shrine, you may also notice many natural positive benefits in other areas of your life. Also, other people may comment that your house always seems peaceful and welcoming!

Sit in a chair with your back straight, but not tense, feet flat on the floor and hands resting in your lap. You can also sit on a floor cushion in a traditional meditation posture. Bring Reiki through during the meditation by placing your hands on the body in a comfortable position, for example, the tops of your legs. Sometimes giving yourself a little Reiki by placing your hands over your heart for a few minutes before meditation can be a good way to calm the mind and get you in the mood for meditation!

To begin, relax your body and focus your mind by mentally scanning your body for tension, and releasing it. Bring your attention to the sensation at the tip of your nostrils. Feel the cool air coming in as you inhale and the warm air going out as you exhale. Concentrate single-pointedly on this sensation. If you get distracted, simply bring your mind back to the object of meditation, the sensation of breathing. This focuses the mind and improves your clarity and concentration. In fact, this simple breathing meditation, if practiced for ten or fifteen minutes daily, can greatly improve our quality of life by giving us a clear and peaceful mind. If we have no experience of meditation, it can be helpful to practice only the breathing meditation for several weeks before trying anything new.

There are two parts to meditation: *Contemplation* and *Placement.* Contemplation is the mental process of abandoning negative thoughts and actions, and of adopting positive ones. When a strong wish arises in the mind to change our behavior for the better, then this is our object of placement and we "hold it" or experience it for as long as possible. For example, if we meditate on the second principle, "Don't worry today," think how worrying in the past has caused much unhappiness and solved no problems. Imagine what it would feel like to completely stop worrying in the future, and how wonderful this would be. *When a strong wish to stop worrying arises in the mind,* "hold" or stay with this mental intention for as long as possible.

If your thoughts wander, simply return to the contemplation until that strong wish to stop worrying arises again, then stay with that feeling or thought. You are actually training yourself to eventually think and feel this way quite naturally. When "holding" the object of meditation, don't strain your mind. It should feel natural, as if your mind has completely mixed or become one with the object of meditation, the wish to stop worrying.

By regularly developing these deep wishes to change for the better, you will definitely become more positive, happy, content, and considerate. This ancient tried-and-tested way of dealing with life's problems, if practiced correctly and regularly, is a guaranteed solution. Unlike other modern methods of finding happiness, addiction to it produces very healthy results!

Use the broad explanations of the Five Reiki Principles (given in chapter 3) as a basis for your meditations. The meditations will be most effective if you apply them directly to your life, based on your own past experiences and understanding. There is no point meditating every day on the vague wish to stop worrying, or to have more respect for others if in your heart you are not really interested in changing, or if these meditations are not directly relevant to your life.

Mentally make the meditations come alive, and then carry your good intentions forward into the rest of your day. Do this by remembering the principle and the positive feelings that arose during your meditation. Try to use this motivation to guide your actions. Whenever you become aware that negative feelings or thoughts, like worry or impatience, are about to arise in your mind, you can prevent them influencing you by recalling your earlier good intentions. In this way, your wisdom will improve, and your daily problems will steadily decrease.

Toward True Wisdom

Wisdom is very different from intellectual ability. Many intelligent people are very unhappy. Since all living beings have the same basic wish to avoid problems and find happiness, wisdom is simply the ability to understand where lasting happiness comes from. As we meditate daily, you will see that happiness is simply a state of mind and that since you have the opportunity to create positive states of mind through meditation, prayer, and Reiki, these methods are the key to lasting happiness. Understanding and acknowledging this is wisdom.

Although the essence and practice of meditation is quite simple, it is a good idea to seek out a fully qualified and experienced teacher who can guide you along the stages of the path of meditation. Learning on your own or from a book, you may encounter many problems and waste much time and consequently lose interest because you don't experience consistently good results. Learning and sharing our experiences with others, meditating in a group, and having the opportunity to ask questions can greatly assist our enjoyment and progress. Having a teacher who is a living example of what we can achieve through meditation is a constant inspiration and encouragement to our own developing practice. (If you want to find a meditation group in your area, see appendices 1 and 3.)

Whatever kind of meditation you choose, if you do a little every day, the good results will grow, you will be more able to relax and enjoy life more fully, and gradually you will become a true source of wisdom, compassion, and inner strength.

10

The Voice of Reiki:

Stories from Reiki Practitioners

Reiki has touched and shaped many lives. Part of the path of Reiki is finding out, from our own experience, how to make the most of this precious gift. We can, however, also learn much from the experience of others.

This book would not be complete without some of the special stories and accounts of Reiki practitioners who have gained great personal benefit from Reiki, and who have taught and treated others successfully. Some of the contributors are friends and students of the author; others simply responded to his invitation to share their wisdom and experience with those walking a similar path.

An Ill Wind That Brought Some Good

by Jean Dunn

I have always been interested in complementary therapies and the spiritual side of life. It was an ill wind that gave me the opportunity to spend more time researching these topics when I was diagnosed and treated for breast cancer in 1995. It was at this time that I became curious about Reiki and I decided to take First and Second Degree.

When I started self-healing I would spend one hour every day and I always felt physically, mentally, and spiritually refreshed after each session. After a few months I reduced the number of sessions to once or twice a week. However, I have now gotten lazy and only practice Reiki when I need it. I don't think this is a good thing and a New Year's resolution for me should be to spend at least one hour each week doing Reiki. I say this because although I now feel as healthy as the next person, I also know when something is missing from my life. After one hour doing Reiki I can feel myself getting more in control, minor aches and pains vanish, and I feel happier and more able to cope with life in general.

I would never mention or discuss matters of a spiritual nature with my husband. He is very "down-to-earth" and doesn't believe in anything like that! However, when I'm thinking, "I must do a Reiki" he invariably says, "Isn't it time you had a Reiki session?" He is aware of the change in me after a treatment!

Looking back, I wish I'd had the time to find Reiki sooner. It's sad that very often we only find something when we need it. If only I'd known and practiced Reiki earlier in life, I might have kept fitter and not had breast cancer. I have however, learned that we should never say, "If only . . . " I can say that Reiki will now always play a part in my life.

Since practicing Reiki, I have been generally a much happier person and feel much more aware of the spiritual side of life and for this I will always be grateful.

Clarity, Wisdom, and Sharing Responsibilities

by Mary Dawson

After months of working, constantly studying, and dividing any spare time between family and friends, I was physically and emotionally drained. I felt used, abused, and unsupported.

I learned and practiced Reiki, hoping it would help me. Reiki helped but not in the way I expected. After self-healing sessions, I would feel stronger, more relaxed, and able to cope for a while, but then the stress and emotional pain would surface again.

One morning in desperation, I sat quietly and asked Reiki for guidance rather than healing, and everything became clear. The problems causing my harassed state were not my problems but another person's.

I was shouldering the responsibilities for someone very close to me. In a misguided way to ease their burden, I was sacrificing my own health and well-being, while at the same time building a wall between us and becoming very bitter at their inadequacies. From then on during my self-healing sessions, I directed Reiki to this person for their "greatest good." The results have been profound for both of us. Hidden fears and realizations have been expressed, attitudes have changed, and trust has been restored. Before this, I think that deep down I was aware of the cause of my dilemma, but unable to deal with it. I chose to ignore it. I truly believe that Reiki brought it out in the open, and showed me my weakness. Not only did Reiki give me the strength to accept and face the problems but also the courage to hand them back to the rightful owner. Now with the help of Reiki I am free to offer love and support to this person while they come to terms with their responsibilities and learn to deal with them, rather than pass them on.

Thank you, Reiki!

A Reason To Be Special

by Ellen Carney

I've been using Reiki for almost a year now, in which time lots of challenging things have happened to me. Without Reiki I'm sure that I would not have dealt with them as calmly as I did. I haven't used Reiki as much or as often as I would like, but it gives a little extra hope to situations when I have used it. When used on friends even the most skeptical cannot help but feel the warmth from what are usually very cold hands, and also relief from sometimes very painful ailments.

It really makes you think about life, how you affect those around you, how others affect you. It makes you aware of just the tiniest things and how important they are. It's given life another reason to be special.

Subtle Changes

by Jean Carney

Reiki has changed my life in very subtle ways. It makes you realize that everything in life has a purpose, even if that purpose is not obvious at the time. Using Reiki for improvement in my own life and that of others can work surprisingly quickly. It has made me much calmer and more tolerant towards the unexpected stresses of everyday life.

The Birth Of A Master

by Barbara Ashworth, Reiki Master

Over the years Reiki kept coming at me, but choosing to put my free will into action I did not do anything about it! I had been working on my spiritual path with a guru, Sri Ravi Shankar, so what did I want with Reiki I thought I was being given everything I needed.

A very dear friend, who had been interested in healing for many years, phoned me one day and asked me if I would like to go with her to a free public talk on Reiki. I thought this might be interesting but had no intention of taking it any further. After the talk we chatted and to our mutual surprise we found that we had both only decided to go because we thought the other wanted to! If we had known this before, we would not have gone! I could not help thinking that although I did not want to do Reiki with the Master who had given the talk, there was a reason for me being there and perhaps there might be a Reiki Master somewhere that was right for me. So I decided that if the right teacher came along, I would do it. I heard about two other Masters but again did not feel drawn to them. Then a friend showed me an advertisement for a Reiki class to be held locally. I phoned the Master to ask more about it; she was very friendly and "down-to-earth." I felt this was just right, so within weeks I was doing First Degree.

At that point in my life I was such a doubter. I needed proof that Reiki worked. I did not have to wait long as one day I slammed the car door on my finger. The pain was unbearable and I immediately gave the finger Reiki. After half an hour there was no pain and the next day there was no bruising, as if it had never happened. A few weeks later I broke my ankle. The doctors decided to use a firm bandage instead of plaster, and I was told not to put any weight on it. I did as I was told and gave it lots of Reiki before my next hospital visit two weeks later. A different doctor saw me this time. He took the dressing off, and there was no bruising . . . I told him I felt no pain. He asked me to wait while he checked the original x-rays, as he did not believe there had been a break. He came back looking very puzzled, as the break was clearly visible on the x-rays! I doubted Reiki no more!

Some weeks later, a friend told me about a man, forty-three years of age who had terminal cancer, and she asked if I would give him some Reiki. I went to see him and gave him Reiki every day for three months. He really loved this and his wife said he always looked forward to his daily treatment. I worked mostly through his hands and feet, and after two weeks he got up from his bed and sat in the garden and began to go for short walks. He was quite well for some time, and was able to go to church to see his young daughters at the harvest festival and travel to Yorkshire to see his mother.

He was very afraid of dying. He thought that he might "go in his sleep" and some nights he could not sleep for the fear, which made his breathing difficult. Sometimes I would stay through the night and give him Reiki, which helped him calm down and begin to come to terms with his situation. The fear was once so intense that I asked my Master to send him some absent healing, which again helped. At this time my Master also suggested I take Second Degree so I could use the symbols to help the man

I was treating. I did not have the money to do this but she taught me anyway knowing that I so much wanted to help him. Learning Second Degree really enhanced my ability to channel Reiki and I am sure this man's transition would have been much more difficult for him and his family if Reiki had not been present.

I began working with Reiki more and more and many people asked me to send them Reiki. One day a close friend asked me to send Reiki to her niece who had broken the tibia in her left leg. A few nights later, my friend phoned to say how delighted her niece was, as the intense pain she had been experiencing had gone and she could walk without crutches. Only then was I told that her leg was so badly broken that it [needed to be pinned] by a surgeon.

I continued with my spiritual practice, which was greatly enhanced by Reiki and I often helped my Reiki Master at exhibitions, as I felt she had given me so much by sharing Reiki with me. At a particular "Mind and Body Exhibition," my Master gave a talk on Reiki and many, many people had come to listen to her. I was astonished at the level of interest in Reiki and I suddenly became aware that there are so many people all over the world who need help and who could benefit from Reiki. Then I had a strong thought from somewhere that said, "Don't you think it is about time that you did your Masters?" At the same time I felt bathed in bliss and I mentally replied, "Yes." After a little while I began to doubt this strong intuition as I knew I would have great difficulty finding the money to become a Master. So I shared my thoughts with a friend and she said, "Don't worry, you know that if the time is right it will just happen." I did know this but hearing it from someone else made me more open to this possibility. After the Master's talk I returned to the stand where we were demonstrating and sharing Reiki with others.

However, I could not shake off the crazy idea that I should actually do my Masters that same day; how this would be possible I did not know.

Later in the day, when it was quieter and I was left alone with my Master she put a chair in front of me and said, "Barbara, there is something I would like to do for you." I sat down in the chair without asking any questions, which is unusual for me! I was aware that she was beginning to attune me and I thought at first it might be another Second Degree attunement. However, after a few minutes I realized it was something much more. I was aware of what felt like a funnel to my right and through this opening groups of symbols were arising and surrounding me. I felt so deeply blessed that I wept from my core. After this Master's attunement I stood up, we hugged, and I cried again!

The next day I talked with my Master again about this experience and she said that shortly before the attunement she had been told by one of her spiritual guides that it was the right time to do the attunement. She said that she thought it was not the right place but again she was told everything would be just right, and subsequently before the attunement the room had become quiet and very peaceful.

I thank Padma O'Gara, my Reiki Master, from the bottom of my heart and I am eternally grateful to the divine Reiki Masters for using me as a channel for Reiki.

There Are No Rules

by Keith Beasley, Reiki Master

A number of Reiki Masters present Reiki as a series of forms to be practiced as they are taught. That—to me—is not in keeping with the spirit of Reiki. Reiki is a living, ever-changing energy, always responding to the reality of the here and now. As such it cannot be defined, it cannot be described in mere words.

My background is in Quality Management. After many years working on standards, I realized that laws, rules, standards, whatever you want to call them, are for those unwilling or unable to think for themselves. Once on the Reiki path, we accept our own responsibility for our life, we move away from needing others to tell us or show us the way to being open to the Universe. Reiki teaches us to see the reality in a given situation and act accordingly. How can any set of written forms or rules allow for all the possible different realities we might face? The authority in Reiki comes not from any association, nor Grand Master, but from Reiki the Energy. Phyllis Lei Furumoto herself admits that, if in doubt, we should listen to our inner voice. The more we do so, the more we trust Reiki, the Universe, our inner/higher self, the more we see that this is the only wisdom there is.

We cling to rules only through fear. We tend to cling to the "shoulds and oughts" that life throws at us because it seems easier. But is it? Not in the long term. As we become more aware through using Reiki, we realize just how many "rules" we allow ourselves to be constrained by. There is so much conditioning. As we use Reiki in our lives, so we let go of the beliefs and dreams and see the cosmic reality. At first, living without the safety net of rules can be scary, but eventually we see that the empty feeling that letting go initially induces leads to the very freedom we seek, the freedom to just "be," to respond with mind, body, and soul to the moment. No rules, no preconceived ideas, expectations, or assumptions, that's what Reiki is about—freeing ourselves from our own mental limitations. Welcome uncertainty into your life . . . it gives the angels a chance to perform miracles.

Reiki And Expectation

by Karen Stratton, Reiki Master

One of the fascinating aspects of Reiki is the fact that it seems to have a mind of its own. The very name Reiki can be translated as "Spiritually Guided Life Force Energy." This really is an appropriate name, as it frequently seems to have a manner of working in ways that are outside of our expectation. This can sometimes be frustrating when we wish to "heal" some specific condition that someone brings to us. I feel that one must always ensure that the recipient realizes that Reiki is not directed by the practitioner and will always work in whatever way is appropriate for the highest good of the individual, and this is often in a way not expected!

In my experience the client often comes for Reiki believing that the symptoms present will hopefully be "cured." I explain that this may not happen. I do firmly believe that the "Inner Practitioner," "Inner Guru," or "Higher Self" will have presented the symptom to ensure that the individual is guided to seek out Reiki. The Reiki will be required at some level of the person's being, maybe for the healing of some other physical condition, or equally often to heal some other aspect of that person's life.

The unexpected things that have occurred in my own experience never cease to amaze and delight me, like the young woman who came for mental/emotional healing, because she was very unhappy. She had very low self-esteem, feeling she was a victim of her circumstances. Over the initial period of six weeks, as she came for regular weekly treatments, something quite unexpected happened. Prior to her starting treatment with me, she had been to see a gynecologist who found that she had a fibroid the size of a billiard ball and needed a hysterectomy. Due to the waiting list in her area, she was told that she would have to wait eighteen months for treatment. Her [general practitioner] then suggested she be seen by a specialist in another authority where the waiting lists were shorter. While waiting for the appointment, she commenced Reiki treatments with me and on the third or fourth session she experienced very powerful surges of energy in her lower abdomen during the treatment, and the next day felt extremely bruised and tender in this area. When she eventually saw the second specialist she was told that, as the fibroid was only the size of a marble, she wouldn't need surgery. Obviously there may be other reasons for this to have happened, but the coincidences seem to indicate it was Reiki! In this lady's case, she also went on to regain her own power beautifully, really taking her life into her own hands in many, many ways.

Another surprise, was a young girl with lupus. She was [overweight] due to water retention. She hated her appearance and was becoming very depressed. Her father asked me if Reiki would help, and I told him I felt sure that she would feel more able to cope with the situation, even if the condition itself didn't change. As soon as she had her first session she began to urinate more frequently than she had for ages, and over the next six sessions of Reiki the water retention simply drained away, leaving her almost back to her normal weight and a very much happier young lady.

Then there was the young lady who, following a serious physical attack upon her person, had been unable to talk about to anyone, and was withdrawn and extremely depressed. I felt that if she had several treatments of Reiki, it would help her to become more relaxed about the feelings and emotions about the situation, and that she would then be able to accept some additional counseling or hypnotherapy to deal with the deeper trauma. To my surprise, however, after only one treatment she was able to pick up the pieces of her life again, and some weeks later needed no further treatments. I realize that she may still need more help in the longer term, but the point is that Reiki worked in an unexpected way yet again.

There are countless examples that could be added to this article, both from personal experience and from that of my students and other Reiki practitioners. We are taught to trust in the innate wisdom of Reiki. It can never do harm and will always work in whatever way is right for the individual's greatest need and highest good. But as humans we sometimes may forget this and can then be guilty of wishing for a specific outcome.

Maybe the lesson here, when we talk of Reiki and what it can do, is to EXPECT THE UNEXPECTED, or probably much more appropriately, HAVE NO EXPECTATION, and let the healing power of Reiki work in its own mysterious and wonderful way.

Reiki At Hand—Melding

by Teresa Collins, Reiki Master

From her book *Reiki At Hand,* published by Collins Press, Ireland

Before I started practicing Reiki, I studied Vispassna Buddhist meditation for two years, and I found this very insightful and helpful when it came to identifying what I was experiencing within myself. I was able to differentiate between what belonged to me and what belonged to the client quite quickly during each Reiki session. It is a great help to actually experience the client's symptoms both from an academic and a humanitarian point of view. Once I recognize that something happening within myself belongs to the client, I thank the energy for bringing this information to my attention and if it does not leave quite quickly, I simply ground it through my grounding cords. If the symptoms stay with me for some time after the session is completed, it is usually something I am healing within myself.

How is it possible for the practitioner to experience the client's symptoms? During a Reiki session the energy of the client and the practitioner becomes one. This means that if the client's mind is overactive, the practitioner's mind will also have a tendency to become overactive. Should the client be depressed, the practitioner may also feel depressed. Should the client have a heart problem, the practitioner may notice his or her own heart behaving strangely. Not every single symptom will be picked up by the practitioner, but only those symptoms that the energy feels is important for the practitioner to be aware of.

Sometimes symptoms are felt by the practitioner that the client is unaware of. Once I treated a woman who had fallen down the stairs the previous night in her sleep, and during the Reiki session I felt quite nauseated. I informed her of this after our session, and told her that she was in shock and that she should go home to bed. She insisted that she was perfectly all right. One hour later she became aware that she was indeed feeling shocked and nauseated and remained so for twenty-four hours. She informed me afterward that she was brought up to be "stoic" and that it was very difficult for her to feel any "weakness" in herself.

The process of the practitioner feeling the client's symptoms is called "melding." No long-term disease or dysfunction may be picked up by the practitioner. For example, if a client comes to the practitioner with arthritis of his or her back, the practitioner may feel the pain in his or her back for a few minutes during the treatment, but will not go on to develop arthritis as a result of giving the treatment.

Self-Healing, Mastery, and Transformation

by Claire M. Ray, BSc.
Usui and Karuna Reiki Master, Seichem Master

In January 1990, I was diagnosed with breast cancer; I was forty-two years old. As soon as I came out of hospital after my mastectomy, a friend took me to a meeting of *Cansurvive,* the English-speaking support group of the Hong Kong Cancer Fund. There a young man was doing a healing on a lady who had lost a leg to bone cancer. After she said, "I feel so much better now," he asked if anyone else was in discomfort. I would have raised my arm if I could, but my twelve-inch scar made it difficult. Over the following weeks, he came to my flat three times to give me Reiki, and also sent distant Reiki twice. When I saw the surgeon again for a check-up, he could not believe how quickly the scar had healed and how little discomfort I had.

In March, a Reiki Master named Esther Valle (now Esther Veltheim) came from Australia and I took Level 1 with her. What a difference Reiki made to my total healing process—I vowed to help as many people as possible with Reiki. In time I went to the UK for two months to renovate my home and had a week at the Bristol Cancer Help Center, a wonderful place full of healing energy and love. Then I had only three days back in Hong Kong before moving, with my husband and daughter, to Singapore. We were still living in the hotel when a fax arrived from Esther saying, "I am arriving next week, do you want to take Level 2?" Of course I did. That was to be the first of the five Level 2 classes I took with different masters over the next three years. In August 1994,

I completed my Masters training with William Rand in Scotland. On the way back to Hong Kong, I stopped in England to teach and attune my mother, aunt, and several friends. I started writing my courses on the long plane journey home and have been teaching Reiki ever since, in Hong Kong, Singapore, the UK, and the USA.

Once a client came to me who had an incurable illness. A Reiki friend and I spent an hour working on him. She sat at his head, and I sat at his feet, doing reflexology and Reiki. For half an hour we saw a stream of golden light running down both sides of his body, and an angel came to his side. When my friend had to leave, the client was asleep, so we left him and tiptoed to the door. About ten minutes later, the music stopped. I noticed the angel had gone down to the client's feet and I left the angel to carry on without my help. After a while, the angel vanished and I rang a Tibetan bell gently to signify the end of the session. When the client awoke a little later, he was astonished to see me by his head, since he thought I was still working on his feet. He could still feel the angel's touch. He is now fully recovered.

Several years ago my elderly father was dying. My mother, aunt, and I were gathered beside his hospital bed, all giving him Reiki through his hands and feet. Suddenly he became restless, as if he was trying to push our hands away. I asked my angels what was the reason, and received the reply that we must let go in order that he can let go and be released from his earthly body. We were holding him to the earth. So we took away our hands and within five seconds his spirit left his body.

The First Time

by Pam Green, Reiki Master

Having worked with the energy of Reiki Master for almost twelve months, I decided I understood enough to feel comfortable in passing on the gift of Reiki to another person. No sooner had I decided I was ready than someone else came to the same conclusion and I met my first student! As she had almost no previous experience of natural healing, we set a steady, gentle pace until the day of her attunement arrived, a first for both of us.

When I placed my hands upon her shoulders to silently ask if she were ready, the tension was obvious. Then there came a loud knock at the front door and I asked to be excused for a moment. I had placed a notice on the door asking not to be disturbed. I opened the door to see a gypsy. Before she could begin the usual rush of words I simply said "I am sorry, I am working." To my surprise, she turned on her heels and almost fled along the path that led to my front door.

When I returned to the Reiki room, I apologized for the interruption and replaced my hands on her shoulders. All the tension had disappeared and she was attuned to First Degree Reiki with the same special gentleness that characterized our meeting . . . Afterwards we spoke of the experience and she confirmed that before the knock on the door she felt her shoulders were around her ears, but that feeling had gone by the time I had returned. When invited to choose something to give her first hands-on healing to, she chose the rather large plant standing in the corner of the Reiki room!

We had arranged to see each other two days later and I couldn't help wondering how she was getting along with

Reiki in her system . . . Saturday had been the day of the attunement. Sunday was her usual wash day and for a person with a family and full-time job outside the home, this always took up a substantial amount of her time. The washing machine refused to work. She was furious.

There was no chance of calling a mechanic. Her husband arrived home from his Sunday lunchtime drink, both unsympathetic and unhelpful . . . she stood in the kitchen wondering what she might do. Then a thought popped into her head, "I know, I'll give it a Reiki treatment." She admitted to feeling extremely ridiculous and not a little embarrassed to be standing in the kitchen with her hands placed on a washing machine inviting Reiki to help her situation.

I wouldn't be telling this story if it didn't have a happy ending! The machine decided to work as long as she needed it on the Sunday, and later that week she called in the more conventional repair service but she considered Reiki had played its part when really needed.

Something she hadn't realized until I told her was that she had given a precious gift to a first-time Reiki Master. I had no need to worry about playing my part on behalf of another person, on behalf of Reiki. I truly felt so blessed for having been given such a fine start to my new career.

Addicted To A Pretty Face

by Keith Beasley, Reiki Master

I decided to take Reiki because I thought it might offer an end to my addictions. I'd realized some years previously that I was far too sensitive to a "pair of sparkling eyes." To receive a kindly smile from any unattached, deep, clear, female eyes was enough to send me falling hopelessly in love. Pathetic really, but when you're brought up on Sunday afternoon romantic films, and you learn that life is about loving and being loved, what else does a single bloke do?

Three years intensive Reiki on myself and teaching it as a Master to others has provided many answers. For one, that there is no simple answer! I'd somehow acquired the idea that romantic love was the only sort. WRONG! Reiki is Love, and can be applied in any and all situations. In my practice of Reiki I found that the act of love, the sharing of Reiki, was fulfilling and wonderful with friends, students, family, nature, myself, and everything else. Slowly I saw that while sharing love with a special lady is the only way of sharing some of the more intimate and intense aspects of Love, there are many, many more ways open to us. The more I shared, the more I received and the less important having a pretty face around became.

Just as important for me was learning the ability to rise above the frustrations of courtship. Reiki, with the help of lady friends, taught me that we can never truly trust another person to satisfy our needs, but we can trust the Universe. When a "loved one" didn't phone, I now had another source of love at hand all the time—Reiki. I wouldn't say the lessons have been easy—far from it—but Reiki has enabled me to face my addiction and work through it so that I can now enjoy being with a pretty face without "going to pieces." Reiki brings that perspective, the wholeness. It helped me to see that, as the great Freddy Mercury sang, "Nothing really matters."

My Reiki Story

by Sheila Sellars D, Hyp. BSch., Reiki Master & Clinical Hypnotherapist

A friend at work, who had the same interests as me and also went to a Spiritualist Church, told me about some

Americans who had visited a local Spiritualist Church some time previous and a form of healing they were teaching called Reiki. I had never heard of it but she said that anyone could do it, which I found a bit hard to believe at the time! This was around 1992.

I started to go to this Spiritualist Church with my friend on a regular basis. We enjoyed the services very much and then one evening they announced that the Americans were coming back again to teach Reiki. A center had been opened quite nearby that was to offer alternative therapies by some of the people involved at the Church and the Americans were to teach Reiki Healing at this center. They had returned to offer the people who had taken First Degree the opportunity of taking Second Degree and some that had taken Second Degree previously were offered the opportunity to take Advanced Reiki. They were also offering First Degree Reiki to new students.

A promotional talk was being given at the center so my friend and I went along to see what it was all about. I was quite impressed by the energy that I could feel and even though I was still a I little skeptical, I decided I would take First Degree, just to see what it was like. I had no intention at that time of taking it any further, little did I know!

I took Reiki First Degree that weekend and was completely amazed at the way I felt. I was on a high after the first morning's tuition. I went back the second day and was still feeling good about it. It opened up a whole new path for me but I hadn't quite realized that then. I started seeing colors I had never seen before with my eyes shut! I had one of the best experiences of my life a week later.

It was decided to present everyone with their certificates at the local Town Hall. This would give people at different levels of Reiki the chance to meet, meditate, and exchange

Reiki. My Reiki Master led us into meditation and I loved the music she had put on, it reminded me of the desert, lots of sand and rolling grass. I was picturing this when I became absolutely freezing cold down one side, the left side I think, my right side stayed the same, then I felt my chair lift off the floor. Of course it didn't, but that's how it felt! Then I saw a Chinese man, a Mandarin I think, who stood behind me but never spoke, he just stood there for a little while. He wore an orange tunic with wide sleeves hanging down. I didn't see his hands as he had them inside his sleeves, he was wearing a hat which went to a short point on the top, with four side panels and was rounded at the sides, a Mandarin's hat, I guess. He wasn't there long but what a brilliant, brilliant feeling it was at the time, something I will never, ever forget. I presume he presented himself to me to be my guide and I thank him greatly for that. I think of him a lot. I call him Mr. Chang, I don't know if that's his correct name but I realize he knows it's me when I talk to him, and he really does help me.

I was really pleased with the energy of the First Degree, so I decided to take Second Degree and again I thought that I wouldn't be taking it any further, for one thing it would be too expensive for me to consider becoming a Master at that time. I did eventually take the Master's Degree, due to a friend who was a medium telephoning me and telling me that her angels had told her that I should do it. Even then I thought about it for quite a while due to the cost but it had become known to her that it was being offered at quite a reduced rate in Glastonbury by another American woman, and so I took the offer up in January 1995. Since then I have seen numerous things and had a few different things happen to me but I can say that I truly am amazed at the progress I feel I have made since taking

Reiki physically, mentally, and spiritually, although I feel I have always been quite spiritual. I use Reiki every day in some form or other.

I have found Reiki to be a wonderful tool in the natural healing process, and that it very subtly guides you along the right path to your destiny. I have since trained many people in this ancient art, and I am always surprised and delighted at their fulfillment and joy in taking the next step in their evolution. I feel a great bond with my students and it's a privilege to teach them.

The attunements, I find, affect people quite differently. Some people see and feel nothing at all at that time and others see and feel lots of different things. I always tell my students that the attunements are personal to them and whatever happens is right for them at that time.

I have treated animals with the energy and find they accept it quite naturally and are seemingly appreciative. They tend to come back for more, and will just wander off when they've had enough!

When my granddaughter was born, her head was a little out of shape because she had been lying in the birth canal for some time. The midwife said it would take around ten weeks for it to go back to normal, so after a couple of weeks I thought I would draw the Reiki symbols over her head and see what happened. Within the week her head had returned to the normal shape. The midwife couldn't believe it! Once again Reiki worked wonders.

Reiki is not always given credit for the good it does. There have been times when people with fixed attitudes have benefited from the energy but given credit to something else. For instance, I have known when someone's breathing has improved and they put it down to the weather! That's fine, what is important is that the person being treated is making progress. We have to learn to be tolerant, everyone is at a different stage in their life program.

I have also found, with Reiki, that I have been led to learn other things, although at the time I didn't quite know where it was all leading to! Things have seemed to simply slot into place when the time is right. I say to those people who are also in this situation, carry on, all will be revealed.

My personal view is that the Reiki energy should be cherished and valued. I cannot agree with the people who think it should cost next to nothing, I do agree the energy should be available to everyone who wants it, but at a cost that helps them to appreciate it, and work with it in a truly loving way.

Reiki has definitely made a difference in my life and in the lives of my students. I think I will always be in awe of the energy.

11

The Good Heart

We are living in times of remarkable opportunities for progress and positive change. Relatively speaking, a few people have a special opportunity to help a great many others.

Reiki is helping to change the world. This silent and peaceful revolution is affecting everyone, not only those who practice Reiki. When we decide to learn and use Reiki regularly, we are doing something very special and meaningful with our lives, something that will also benefit many generations to come.

As we develop our intention to walk the path of living Reiki toward wisdom and self-awareness, as Dr. Mikao Usui did, so the whole world will become a more peaceful, nurturing, and supportive community. As more people wish to carry the light of Reiki, regardless of race or religion, and motivated by the wish to benefit others, as Dr. Usui was, so this light will spread and touch the hearts and minds of all living beings, helping to eventually bring an end to ignorance, oppression, and suffering wherever they appear to exist.

There are many paths to personal growth, healing, and inner happiness. Reiki is one of them and can enhance all of them. Reiki thrives on honesty, a good heart, and a willingness to learn. If you want to gain the most from Reiki, just be yourself, follow your heart, learn from your own experience, and Reiki will bring the path up to meet you. Personal experience of Reiki is much more valuable than any attempt to explain its origins or categorize it. Use it. Play with it. Share it. Make mistakes with it. Only in this way will you discover your own potential, and the opportunity that Reiki offers you for becoming all that you are.

All the answers to all the problems we will ever encounter are held within our own mind. With the will to change, we can use Reiki to tap into the infinite resources we hold within us and gradually peel away the layers of misunderstanding and confusion that color the way we view "reality."

Buddha taught that "everything depends upon the mind." We can say that happiness depends upon the mind, not on external factors. Understanding this simple truth is the key to solving all our problems. If we begin to walk this path of understanding, with the help of Reiki, it will lead us to greater and greater contentment, inner peace, and the ability to truly benefit others. Nothing is more precious than the wish to change for the better and to improve the quality of our own and others lives by realizing our own true nature.

The main wish of all living beings is to find lasting happiness. If we pursue our goal of complete happiness from within, motivated by the wish to share this infinite wealth with others, there can be no higher purpose to our lives. This is living Reiki.

Dedication

To the Greatest Good for all living beings.

Appendix 1: Meditation

The demand for a lasting solution to the problems of stress and anxiety created by the nature of today's "material" society has led to the setting up of meditation groups in almost every town and city. These groups vary in content and in their spiritual origin, so it is important to find one that you feel comfortable with, one that is run by a fully qualified teacher and one that teaches a recognized and correct path true to the origins of meditation.

Buddhist Meditation

Most meditation groups can trace their origins back to Buddha, who lived over 2,000 years ago. He was born into one of the richest and most powerful royal families in India and spent the first twenty-nine years of his life living as a prince. However despite having all the health, wealth, and good relationships he could wish for, he still felt incomplete and he could also see a great need in others for a real solution to life's problems. Finally he came to understand that most people look for happiness in the wrong place! He felt sure that true lasting happiness could be found simply by understanding and developing the mind. He decided to give up his inheritance and devote the rest of his life to attaining the ultimate state of wisdom and happiness, so that he could share this with others. All Buddha's teachings were recorded and passed down and to this day we have a pure, unbroken lineage of the path to full enlightenment.

New Kadampa Tradition

The New Kadampa Tradition (NKT) is one of the largest international Buddhist organizations. Established in 1976 by Tibetan meditation master Geshe Kelsang Gyatso Rinpoche, its purpose is "to present the mainstream of Buddhist teachings in a way that is relevant and immediately applicable to the contemporary Western way of life." Most cities and towns in the UK have an NKT residential center or meditation group and many others are opening in the USA, Europe, and elsewhere. (See appendix 2 for books by Geshe Kelsang Gyatso on Buddhism and Buddhist practice.) To find your nearest Buddhist center, or if you would like a teacher to give an introductory talk on Buddhism in your area, please contact:

Main Contact:
New Kadampa Tradition
Conishead Priory
Ulverston
Cumbria
England
LA12 9QQ
TEL/FAX: 01229 588533 (within UK)
E-mail: HYPERLINK mail to: kadampa@dircon.co.uk
World Wide Web site: http://www.kadampa.net

In the USA contact:
Kadampa Tradition
Kadampa Meditation Center
47 Sweeney Rd.
P.O. Box 447
Glen Spey, NY 12737
TEL: (914) 856-9000
TOLL FREE: 1-877-KADAMPA (1-877-523-2672)
E-mail: KadampaCenter@aol.com

Appendix 2: Books on Buddhism

All the following books are written by Geshe Kelsang Gyatso and published by Tharpa Publications.

For beginners and experienced practitioners:

Buddhism: A Beginner's Guide

Introduction to Buddhism: An Explanation of the Buddhist Way of Life

The Meditation Handbook: A Practical Guide to Meditation

Universal Compassion: Transforming Your Life Through Love and Compassion

Eight Steps to Happiness: The Buddhist Way of Loving Kindness

Joyful Path of Good Fortune: The Complete Buddhist Path to Enlightenment

Meaningful to Behold: The Bodhisattva's Way of Life

There are many other more advanced and in-depth titles on Buddhism available from Tharpa Publications. They also produce Buddhist art reproductions, tapes, talking books, and books in Braille. To obtain a brochure, please contact:

In the UK:
Tharpa Publications
Kilnwick Percy Hall
Pocklington
York, YO4 2UF
United Kingdom
TEL: 01759 306446
FAX: 01759 306397
E-mail: HYPERLINK mail to: tharpa@tharpa.com
World Wide Web site: http://www.tharpa.com

In the USA:
Tharpa Publications
P.O. Box 1104
Haddonfield, NJ 08033-1044
TEL: (609) 869-0903
FAX: (609) 869-4858
E-mail: tharpaus@aol.com
World Wide Web site: http://www.tharpa.com

Tharpa Publications also have offices and outlets in many other countries.

Appendix 3: The Reiki Association and Reiki Alliance

The Association provides a quarterly magazine, information about local Reiki Exchanges and other events in the Reiki community, a Reiki Helpline, and Reiki Outreach International, which was set up to organize group absentee healing for world situations such as famine, war, poverty, and other global conflicts, crises, or "issues."

The Reiki Association
Cornbrook Bridge House
Clee Hill
Ludlow
Shropshire,
England SY8 3QQ
TEL/FAX: 01584 891197
E-mail: HYPERLINK mail to:
reikiassoc_admin@compuserve.com

The Reiki Alliance
P.O. Box 41
Cataldo, ID 83810 USA
TEL: (208) 682-3535
FAX: (208) 682-4848
E-mail: 75051.3471@compuserve.com

The Reiki Alliance
Postbus 75523 1070 AM
Amsterdam
Netherlands
TEL: 31 20 6719276
FAX: 31 20 6711736
E-mail: 100125.466@compuserve.com

U.K. Reiki Federation
P.O. Box 261
Wembley, HAO 4FP
England
E-mail: enquiry@reikifed.co.uk
World Wide Web site: reikifed.co.uk

Index

A

B

C

H

I

J

K

L

M

N

P

R

U

W

Y